A Long, Long, Long, Journey

A Century of Memories

by John B. Smith

PORTLAND • OREGON
INKWATERPRESS.COM

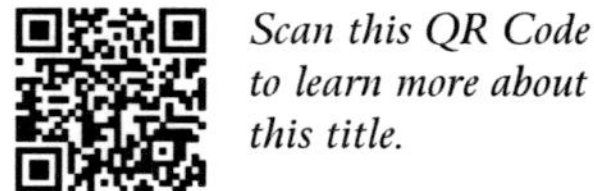

Publisher: Inkwater Press | www.inkwaterpress.com

Paperback
ISBN-13 978-1-62901-100-4 | ISBN-10 1-62901-100-2

Hardback
ISBN-13 978-1-62901-101-1 | ISBN-10 1-62901-101-0

Kindle
ISBN-13 978-1-62901-109-7 | ISBN-10 1-62901-109-6

Printed in the U.S.A.
All paper is acid free and meets all ANSI standards for archival quality paper.

1 3 5 7 9 10 8 6 4 2

Dedication

I dedicate this "autobiography" to my present wife, Grace, who has been an angel since our marriage;

To my first wife, Ruth Elizabeth, to whom I was married for 68 years;

To my mom and dad, who did an excellent job of setting high standards and raising us three boys;

To those who, in one way or another, went out of their way to assist me and Grace in putting things together to make this project a factual, historical record of my life.

Heigh! To a Lifelong Journey

i saw you on horseback
beneath a vast space of blue,
erect and proud and sleek,
your eyes lassoed to a beacon
on the far glistening horizon …
you caught the faint slice of smile
on my face as i stood barefoot
by the wayside under the glaring sun.
and i soon hearkened to a song
inviting my heart to a tandem ride
for a long long journey with you
on this wondrous trail of life.

—grace d. smith

Table of Contents

Dedication iii

Poem: Heigh! To a Lifelong Journey v

Acknowledgements ix

Preface xi

Introduction xxi

Chapter I: The Earliest Days of My Life 1

Chapter II: Life in the Umpqua Forest 21

Chapter III: Forest Service Career 27

Chapter IV: Year 1935 and Thereafter 41

Chapter V: Lakeview Willamette and New Chiefs 57

Chapter VI: Wallowa-Whitman, Washington,
    D.C., Alaska, and Denver 71

Chapter VII: Retirement 83

Chapter VIII: In All 93

Chapter IX: Timber Wolves, Grizzly Bears,
    Cougars: Bad Neighbors 115

Addendum 121

Photos 123

Poem: Crossing the Bar 137

Jack Smith—RFD 139

Acknowledgements

Grace and I would like to acknowledge my son, John, who acts as trustee, comes twice a week, and keeps my business assets current and healthy.

Nathan Han, a grandson and co-trustee, assists by keeping track of many other positive things.

Granddaughter Andrea, born in a military hospital in Germany, comes once a week, usually Saturday, for two hours or more to visit.

Granddaughter Taya is very busy, but she comes several times a month to brighten our lives and brings grandchildren Bodhi and Taeva.

With some close friends and family, including in-laws, we are never short of visitors. All my descendants are supportive, for which I thank them all.

Preface

As I write this, I am 99½ years old, 50 days short of 100. Grace, my present wife, keeps me healthy by watching my diet, encouraging me to exercise, tending to my other care needs at home, and driving me where I need to go. *This is a blessing.* My left eye is blind and my right eye has dimmed to where I don't drive anymore. Although I have lived many places, I have kept an Oregon driver's license since 1929. I have driven two million miles without significant accident. Grace P. Diaz and I were married February 14, 2009. I was lonely and she has just been the angel I needed.

My 35 years with the USDA Forest Service were never easy, always worthwhile, and usually challenging. I worked for and with some of the greatest people to be found anywhere. I enjoyed Ollie Peters' report on the tenure at Silver Lake Ranger Station. I was an assistant ranger at Bly Ranger District and ranger of Drews Valley District during those years.

My family, totaling eight, moved from Texas to Perdue (later Milo), Oregon, in 1915, when I was two years of age. We were a working family. My dad, Jacob Samuel Smith, Sr., built homes, barns, and bridges and farmed. My mother looked after the family—her parents, a foster daughter, and us three boys. She was a great pioneer lady. Her attitude was always, "If someone else can do it, I should be able to do it, and maybe I can do it better."

Amos Buker was postmaster at Perdue. When he took on the 1920 census, he violated his postmaster agreement by having two government jobs, so the Post Office Department closed the post office. I well remember my mother carrying petitions around the community in a horse and buggy, with us three boys as passengers, to get the post office back in business, and she did, only it had a name change—Milo.

Dad built the first Forest Service warehouse at the Tiller Ranger headquarters in the early to mid-1920s. The warehouse had a frost-proof room for canned goods and space for fire tools and equipment for 200 firefighters. He also built several log stringer bridges on the South Umpqua Road between Salt Creek and

Boulder Creek—a distance of some 12 to 15 miles. Douglas fir trees were felled and peeled for stringers. They were yarded and placed with a team of horses. Decking was usually sawn timber, and running planks were added for the vehicles to use in crossing the bridge.

My oldest brother, Dub, was the primary assistant to the ranger from the mid-twenties into the early thirties. Jake, my other brother, who was two years older than me, started on the Tiller District in 1928. In 1932, he supervised a crew of about 15 men—locating and building trail along Jackson Creek, from the South Umpqua River to the Rogue-Umpqua Divide, a distance of 35 miles. In 1935, I did "betterment work" on this heavily used trail with a four-man crew. We felled "pack bumper" trees and blasted slick bedrock, making the trail safer and more usable. We also maintained the side trails. We did one overnight at squaw flat, a large, wet meadow. Mosquitoes were numerous and hungry, so no one slept.

As a younger brother, I hung around where my dad and brothers worked some of the time. I played the old time fiddle tolerably well and often provided music at the meetings after dinner. If Carl Neal, the forest supervisor, happened to be at the meeting, he always gave me a flowery introduction. The men enjoyed the music, and sometimes they sang along.

Pie socials were another social event when I was growing up in Perdue, Oregon. Each girl would bake a pie and describe to her special boyfriend what the package holding the pie looked like so he could bid on it. If he won the bidding, he got to eat dinner, including the pie, with his girlfriend. There would be two or three of these pie socials during the school year.

Bear fat was popular with the housewives for making pie crusts. When rendered, the fat did not set up solid like lard or tallow, but was semi-liquid. They said the pie crust, if made with bear fat, always was tender, and the consumer always bragged about it.

I started fighting forest fires, almost always with an experienced neighbor, for Douglas County Fire Protection Association when I was 13 or 14 years of age. I hired on at the Tiller District in 1930 when I was 16 years of age. Frank and Hugh Ritter were the forest rangers during those years. I became a skilled smoke chaser and forest firefighter early in my Forest Service career. I also planned, scheduled, and managed at least a dozen fire guard training schools on several forests during the 1930s, 1940s, and 1950s.

There were several mineralized areas in our part of Douglas County and always a few prospectors looking to develop a mine. We knew some of them and they sometimes stayed at our house.

Elmer Brooks was from Seattle and he stayed with us when prospecting. He put in some time at "Shively," some ten miles by trail from our place. Several prospectors worked at Shively. They thought the white metal was "silver," but the assays came back negative .Twenty years or so later, a French company, which had the know-how to extract nickel, came to Douglas County and operated on nickel near Riddle, Oregon. The ore gave out after some 25 years, and they also used the top of Quartz Mountain, some 50 miles distant, in the extraction process. The white metal was nickel, but there was not sufficient ore at Shively to encourage them to develop a plant there.

Coffee Creek, which enters the South

Umpqua River between Milo and Tiller, has had placer gold mining during my lifetime.

At the head of Salt Creek, above Tiller, there is a quicksilver mine that has operated off and on through the past 100 years.

And we have our "lost mine." It is the Schieffelin mine at the head of Days Creek.

In 1939, I married Ruth Elizabeth Lange. We had our two girls, Jan (deceased) and Jenny (deceased), and a son, John William, now 68 years of age. I completed a BS in Forest Management at Corvallis. I also took the Junior Forester exam (JF) and passed it, when only one of six who took it passed. The US Government didn't need foresters, so they cranked out a tough examination. With my 10 years of experience, good recommendations, and having passed the JF, I was qualified and became a full-time civil service employee on the Umpqua National Forest.

I was busy on the Umpqua Forest in timber management when the Japanese attacked Pearl Harbor on December 7, 1941. As the war advanced, there was an increased need for timber. It seemed as though we were always short of people, but we put up the sales, supervised the harvest, disposed of the slash, and reforested the areas. We also did a good job of fire protection.

I remember controlling several lightning fires on the Bly District, Fremont Forest, as a lone firefighter. I went from one fire to the next and controlled all of them—they never escaped and spread. I worked from 3:00 p.m. until 11:00 a.m. the next morning, when I was able to pick up Ole Brubeck, a grader man, to help with the last fire. It was probably half an acre when we got to it. The day was heating up, the wind was getting stronger, and the fire wanted to burn. We threw dirt, dug fire line, and got singed, but we controlled the fire. The extra effort we made prevented Fish Hole Mountain from burning.

As many of you US Forest Service retirees know, I had a great career—35 years in the US Forest Service.

Nonetheless, I had very interesting hobbies in the evenings and nights. When I was a CCC foreman at Steamboat, some of the best rainbow trout and summer steelhead fast water was close by in the North Umpqua River. The first artificial fly I tied caught a 12-inch trout. I ordered fly tying supplies from Herter's and copied commercial varieties. They all caught trout. I designed a fly I called "a bucktail caddis" that caught big trout everywhere, and I still have my fly tying equipment.

When I was in the Wallowa National Forest, I had access to Wallowa Lake, which had rainbow trout and landlocked sockeye salmon. It was there I built my first outboard runabout, which performed well. Over the years I built three outboard runabouts, the largest of which I used on saltwater in Juneau, Alaska.

While at Baker, I had good deer, elk, and bird hunting. I got some instruction books and reloaded both rifle and shotgun shells; all worked well.

While I was assigned in Washington, D.C., I built a boat to use in Chesapeake Bay, and I made a coffee table with a glass covered top as a showcase for the arrowheads I had collected when I was a kid.

Shortly after retirement, I got some mushroom books and started gathering mushrooms. I learned six or eight edible varieties of mushrooms, which I still gather.

Hobbies are relaxing and good for your mental health as you consider tough decisions on the job.

Looking back, I don't see how it could have been any better.

I have stayed busy in forest ownership and management since retirement from the Forest Service on June 1, 1970. At age 99½, I feel good, sleep well, eat well, and help my neighbors. I seem to have fairly good recall, memory, and intellect. I walk without a cane. I lost Ruth, my first wife, of almost 70 years, in 2007. We had a top of the line marriage for 68 years.

Introduction

Jacob Smith was born near Hanover, Germany, about 1809. His wife, Katharin, was born in 1794 in Germany. She died in Missouri, January 30, 1890, and he died February 1, 1890. They are buried together in the churchyard at Antioch, Missouri. Their son, William Kyle Smith, was born in Saline County, Missouri, in 1831 and died at Sweet Springs on August 5, 1921. Kyle married Mary Elizabeth Kester, who was born on December 29, 1845, and died in 1925.

Their son, Jacob Samuel Smith, Sr., my father, was born December 25, 1869, and died in November 1934. He married Florence Anna Todd, born in November 1883 in Merle, Texas, and died in Eugene, Oregon, May 21, 1975. Jacob and Florence are buried at Canyonville Masonic Cemetery in Canyonville, Oregon.

Florence's parents were Cyrus Bridges Todd, born February 4, 1846, in Missouri and Mary Creola Anderson, born June 9, 1860, in French Camp, Mississippi. Mr. Todd died April 4, 1922, and Mary Creola died September 7, 1922. They are buried at the Masonic Cemetery in Canyonville. Cyrus' dad was Abia Paric Todd, born February 1, 1817, in Kentucky and died January 8, 1848. He married Mary Ann Bridges; their son was my grandfather, Cyrus Bridges Todd.

I WANT TO SHARE THIS NUGGET OF INFORMATION from my grandparents' experiences:

Grandfather Smith and Grandfather Todd were both in the Confederate Army, Grandfather Smith in the cavalry and Grandfather Todd in the infantry. They were both born in Missouri. They did not have slaves and they did not believe in slavery. However, the Northern Army established military camps in Missouri and took some of their pureblood livestock and butchered them for food. So both my grandfathers joined the Missouri State Guard. Very soon, they were taken into the Confederate Army and fought with the Confederate Army all the way to Louisiana, where they surrendered. They had to sign a pledge that they would not fight anymore, were given a saddle horse and a weapon and told they could go home.

Grandfather Smith went back to Missouri, travelling on horseback alone. Grandfather Todd was sleeping on the ground with his saddle horse's reins around his wrist. The horse whinnied and awoke him. He spotted another saddle horse and a man with a revolver sneaking toward him. He rolled over and cocked his Sharps rifle. The intruder heard the hammer click, and he turned and ran to his horse and galloped away.

Grandfather Todd continued to Burleson County, about 100 miles north of Houston, where he got a job on a cattle ranch. It was there where he met Mary Creola Anderson, married her, and settled down.

A LONG, LONG JOURNEY

CHAPTER I

The Earliest Days of My Life

I am John B. "Jack" Smith. I was born in Olustee, Jackson County, Oklahoma, on the Salt Fork of the Red River, November 19, 1913. My father, Jacob Samuel Smith, Sr., moved the family to Roseburg, Oregon, in 1915. My full given name is "John Benjamin Smith" and I have been called "Jack Smith" by friends since I was a small child. My folks had a little problem finding a name for me, and when I ordered my birth certificate a few years ago, it listed me as Baby Smith, but the date, November 19, 1913, for my birthdate was right, so I am John Benjamin Smith. My uncle had the name John, and my ancestors go back to the early days of the US when it was a colony of England, and some of their ancestors were high on Benjamin Franklin, and the name Benjamin shows in my ancestry down through the years. As for my nickname, I think it was common 90 years ago or so for the name "Jack" to be used as a substitute for John.

I was a crawler at one year of age. I found a copper penny on the floor. When I tried to swallow it, I choked. My dad turned me upside down and shook me. Out came the penny, and it was a keepsake for some years as I was growing up!

When I was two years of age, my dad moved the family to Roseburg, in Douglas Country, Oregon, leaving the drought and Dust Bowl behind, and bought a small farm at the mouth of Stouts Creek, some 20 miles east of Canyonville, Oregon, on the South Umpqua River.

My dad had skills; he built bridges, residences, barns, etc., while my mother and her parents, Cyrus and Creola, ran the farm and raised us three boys, all of whom were born in Oklahoma.

When we got settled into the loggers' shack at Perdue, Oregon, we had big cast iron heating stove in the living room in the winter. It kept the house warm. Sometimes we sat around it in the evenings and cracked and ate walnuts and hickory nuts. Grandfather Smith, in Missouri, would send us a gunny sack of black walnuts and hickory nuts each winter. Sometimes I would open the front door of the stove and play in the fire with paper or sticks of kindling, watching the flame. Mother told me to quit playing in the fire. When I didn't promptly pay attention to her, she went to get her switch, which really stung when she pulled down our pants and used it on our bare butts. Dub, who was five years older than me, quickly hoisted me on his back with my arms around his neck and told Mother I was too small to be switched, that he would look after me and be sure I didn't play in the fire, so I escaped a good switching, but I couldn't play in the fire after that incident.

When I was about five years old, I used to ride the tail end of the tops of second growth trees as my dad pulled them down a hill with a mule team and a dolly to the sawmill. He taught me the right way: Always jump backwards and get off of the log so you don't get hurt. But I really enjoyed that when I was just a little kid.

In 1920, I started first grade in the Perdue one-room schoolhouse, which was across the river and upstream, about half a mile's walk from our home, Granddad Cy Todd and Grandma Creola taught me my ABCs and my 123s, so my mind was wide open to what the teacher, Minnie Thompson, was teaching the other kids. I was especially interested in geography, and I learned those lessons in my first and second grades from the older kids who were in the geography class. In all, there were about 15 kids in the one-room school.

Minnie was my foster sister and later married Jehu Wright. Her parents died of a malady common to the South and she was an orphan. My mother took her in and adopted her, and she became an important part of the family, helping us kids as we grew up. Dad sent her through teachers' college in Oklahoma, and she taught one year of school there before coming to Oregon, where she lived with us until she got married. Because of my open mind, I learned much of the higher classwork from the teacher and other Thompson students. The school was closed and in 1922 we rode the school bus some nine miles to the Consolidated Days Creek High School. The country road was full of chuck holes, but we got there. At Days Creek School, they gave me an examination and put me in the fourth grade. I graduated from Days Creek High School when I was 15 years of age. At Days Creek High School, I played basketball and baseball. I was quick, but too small to be a very good basketball player. I pitched or played shortstop on the high school baseball team. I had a good variety of curve pitches, but could not throw a good fastball. Most of the time I was leadoff batter and would get a hit or a walk.

When I was eight years of age, my two older brothers told me it was time for me to learn how to swim. They said, "We will take you up the South Umpqua River to the bluff and show you how." So they took me up the river to the bluff and demonstrated to me how to do it. There was a deep channel on the south side of the river, next to a ledge above deep water. One at a time, they climbed up on a ledge with me between them and pushed me into the deep channel. I was scared. There was a current and a deep hole close by, downstream, so I had to angle upstream so the current would assist me across the deep channel. I swam dog fashion and made the water fly. I got across the deep channel. As time went by, I practiced and became a very good swimmer.

When I was ten years of age, Mom and Dad applied to the state of Oregon for a water right to Stouts Creek to irrigate the farm and received it. Dad engineered the ditch; it required a low dam at the forks about one mile up the Stouts Creek from our place, which would allow us to irrigate most of the farmland, so we surveyed the location of the ditch and dug it with pick and shovel. We also flumed canyon crossings where necessary. We had a revolving screen at the intake so fish would not go down the ditch and so we could find a leak and plug it. A little ditch maintenance was required every year, but irrigation really increased our yields. Our farm had been an old Indian camp for eons. After tilling and a good rainstorm, Jake and I could fill a full cigar box's worth of Indian artifacts, such as arrowheads, spearheads, scrapers, and drills. This was probably a yearlong camp. Deer and elk were plentiful, as were salmon and trout. Also, blue grouse, ruffed grouse, mountain quail, band-tailed pigeons, and mourning doves. Wild ducks and geese were also there in the spring and fall, during migration periods.

When I was about 11 years old, the following anecdote became very popular. It was about a certain "Mr. Jones," who was a Rogue River character and storyteller who used to show up in Canyonville, Oregon, at rare intervals when I was a small boy. He would head for Bob Couglar's barber shop for a haircut, shave, and shower. Bob was a local barber for 50 years or more, and most barber shops in the 1920s provided a shower for people to clean up. A lot of the individual residences did not have running water, and some lived in the backcountry, so when they got to town, they needed to clean up. It was acknowledged around town that Mr. Jones entertained the small crowd at the barber shop with an outrageous story and then visited a certain house in town for female company before going back to his cabin in the lower Rogue River country. His story on one particular trip went about like this:

"I had ridden on this particular trip on a spot called the 'Teetering Rock' many times, but had never taken the time to get off 'Old Nell.' My saddle horse walked over to the rock and I examined it closely. In this particular trip, it looked to me that I might be able to push it hard enough to get it started rolling down the hill towards the Rogue River. So I got my back against it and pushed hard, but nothing happened. So I changed my location and pushed hard again. It moved a little, so I got my back against it and my legs bent at the knees and gave a mighty push.

"Slowly, Teetering Rock started rolling toward the Rogue River. It made a mighty splash when it hit the Rogue River and several salmon flew through the air. The rock continued up the hill to the opposite bank. Then it slowed, stopped, and here it came back down the hill it went up. I had to get out of the way, but then back down the hill it went. I had been away from my cabin several days, so I left. When I came back to look just before dark, there was a deep gouge where the rock had been going back and forth all day. Teetering Rock itself had worn down to a small, round rock about the size of a baseball but was still going back and forth."

I belonged to Toastmasters International Club in Eugene for six years and used the above story to win their Liar's Contest one year.

I started working on the Clough Ranch in the summer when I was 12 years of age. I got the same wages they paid other ranch employees and my board and room, but it varied during prune harvest. They treated me well and invited me to attend some of their planning and financial meetings. I learned a lot from them.

We bought a small farm (approximately 40 acres). I think it was a fascinating place for us boys to grow up. There had been a water power sawmill on the five-acre flat near Stouts Creek that the Burdines had operated. There was a lower dam for log storage and an upper dam to get a head of water to run the mill. The mill had been salvaged and probably moved somewhere else, but the lower dam and mill pond were intact. The upper dam was some three-eighths of a mile up the creek, but the dam, when we arrived, would not hold water. The creek ran through the remains of the old structure. However, the ditch, some four feet wide, that carried the water around the hillside to power the mill, was there. The ditch carried water to a penstock, which gave a head of 50 feet or more to power the mill.

Many old tools and metal parts from the mill were scattered around the mill site, and we three boys always found something new as play thing. This part of Stouts Creek was always a good place to catch large trout. The creek also had large runs of Coho salmon. Some spawning salmon always make it past the dams and up the creek. Steelhead also ran Stouts Creek.

Many of the old growth Douglas fir trees that were harvested were six feet to eight feet DBH (diameter at breast height). The larger ones were either too big for the sawmill or too heavy to skid, so the loggers used their springboards and felled them some 20 feet above the surface of the ground. We felled the stubs and made firewood of them, and my dad spent a lot of time blasting, sawing, burning, and chopping to get rid of the stumps and to make farmland.

There was little in the way of improvements on the place when we acquired it. There was a dug well and a loggers' shack with several rooms, and our family of eight occupied it after doing some remodeling. Every member of the family worked. We felled cedar trees and made posts and split picket and fenced the whole farm. This was a necessity to keep the numerous black-tailed deer from eating the crops. We always had plenty to eat: venison, trout, steelhead, spring Chinook salmon, and sea run cutthroat trout. We also had fruits, such as cherries, berries, peaches, and apples. Our dining table seated 12 and the chairs were often all occupied at mealtime. Mother was a good cook.

Dad always had a team of horses or mules. We built a big barn with stalls for four horses, stanchions for six cows, an upper level hay mow, and storage for grain and equipment on the main level. There was a big shed on one side of the barn for loose livestock. We also had a chicken house and several other out-buildings. We raised turkeys, ducks, chicken, sheep, and hogs. Most years, we raised a steer for home use and we milked three or four Jersey cows. The first few years, we had a buggy horse; most years, Dad leased some good farmland for cornfields. He raised 30 to 40 pigs a year and fattened them with corn. After several years, we replaced the picket fence with woven wire.

We bought a 1917 Ford Model T touring car, and not long after, we purchased a Fordson Tractor. Our farm was on the south side of the South Umpqua River. The county road, now a forest highway, was on the north side. There was a country store and the Perdue Post Office (later Milo Post Office). We had to ford the river with a team of horses and a wagon, and almost always had a boat. We three boys learned to row at an early age. We stayed off the river when it was high.

Dad built a footbridge (called a swinging bridge) across the South Umpqua River in 1923. This bridge washed out in February 1927. We built it back in the same place. In 1934, the anchor failed on the north side, causing the bridge deck to slope downriver. The bridge was still useable but not really safe, especially when it was wet. In the spring of 1935, my brother Jake and I moved the location downstream a short distance and rebuilt the bridge. The bridge lasted until 1967, when a great storm came up the Pacific coast and the river reached an all-time high. Dad and I built a new house in 1928 and 1929, replacing the old loggers' shack. We also dug a new well 27 feet to bedrock.

In 1924 and 1925, Dad leased a farm in Orchard Valley in Canyonville, and we boys went to Canyonville School (7th and 8th grades). Dub was on the debating team and did very well.

While in Canyonville School, I had a good buddy named Robert Schaffer. His family started Gospel Mission Academy. I still have members of the family, Bob and Laura Dunbar, as close friends.

Jake and I had good jobs in 1929, so we didn't start college until January 1930. By the end of winter term, we went home to Milo, as the great depression was on.

During the school year, Jake and I trapped furs. We caught minks, coons, skunks, civets, ringtail cats, coyotes, and bobcats. We trapped up to the creeks and down the ridges, running the traplines with a lantern at night and on weekends. We probably had 15 miles of trapline. We saw no deer, a sign they had either been eaten by wolves or moved to a higher elevation.

Dub died in 1933 from an accidental gunshot. My dad died from a heart attack in 1934. Mother sold the farm in 1936. She kept house for Jake for a couple of years. He married in 1936, and she moved to an apartment in Eugene, where she lived until her death in 1975, at the age of 92. She was a great pioneer lady. She and dad helped others. Their romance lasted for 26 years, until his death. We did not have electricity while we lived on the farm. It came in 1937.

When we were young, mother canned two

black-tailed deer bucks yearly and corned a couple. We ate the corned first. Dad made a 40-gallon crock of sauerkraut in the fall, and we also had plenty of hams and bacon to last until the next season. Dad used an old German recipe to cure ham and bacon, and they were really good.

The South Umpqua River has a steep gradient and is a beast at flood stage. We stayed away from it when it was high. We knew the level where we could cross it with a team and wagon, or a saddle horse, or in a boat. The bodies of those who tried to cross when it was flooding were often found 30 to 40 miles downriver after the flood was over. We always took home enough staple supplies, such as flour and sugar to carry us through the winter.

Dad was a good farmer. We did not have commercial fertilizer. We used barnyard manure. He could harvest up to 100 bushels of corn per acre on good river-bottom soil. He always picked his seed corn from the previous year's crops.

The stock market crashed October 1929, and most businesses held on to their money and quit hiring. Employment crashed, and there were few jobs. Herbert Hoover and

Calvin Coolidge were blamed for the crash, but it was worldwide. President Franklin D. Roosevelt was elected in 1932, and he started the CCC (Civilian Conservation Corps), which established 200-man camps of enrollees to employ young men and stimulate the economy. The camps were established in rural areas, and the young men were trained in conservation works, primarily on national and state forests. The enrollees received $5 and their housing, food, and clothing, and another $25 went to their families. I was an enrollee early in the program and later on became a foreman. It was an excellent program for the times. Millions of young men were enrolled and trained. The good food in the camps helped many of them grow from boys to men. There was what they called incentive enrollees, who as assistant leaders got $11 per month and as leaders, $15 per month. Many skilled and experienced and capable people did not have work, so they were available as foremen.

Academically, I made good grades in high school and graduated in 1929. Right out of high school, I caught a bus to Aunt Lu's mining claims on the Shasta River in northern California.

The bus stopped in Grants Pass, where I spent the night. I had my first experience with bedbugs. I didn't get much sleep. I killed bugs all night. The next morning, I rode the bus to the mining claims. I stopped the bus at the Shasta River, waded the river, and was greeted by Aunt Lu and her husband, Pat Barnun. (Aunt Lu was a relative of the Clough family and I had met her at the Clough Ranch.) They had a cabin for me, and I could make depression wages, one dollar a day. I found a spot that the Chinese miners had missed some 60 years earlier, where I got an ounce of coarse gold in one gold pan of gravel. At that time, gold was selling at $17 an ounce.

Pat owned seven acres some 60 miles away on a back channel on the Klamath River. In late summer, we moved there. Pat had a nice cabin, and we drove a tunnel into a back channel. We hit river gravel and took some $2,000 in gold on the edge of the channel. We immediately put that into equipment we needed to have a good operation. I worked with Pat, an experienced miner, and learned how to timber a tunnel and work relatively safely underground, but we never found anything as good as where we made our first strike. I missed my family and friends in Oregon, was homesick, and went home in March after several months of tunnel mining. Pat went to Oakland, California, and had a job in the shipyards, but he failed to answer my letters. Something must have happened to him. He was a fine gentleman and a good friend.

As a little boy, I always looked forward to the hog butchering. It always started with a good fire going under the vat to get the water hot so the hogs could be scalded. When the water was hot, a pig would be brought to the vicinity of the vat, where he was shot with a .22 caliber in the forehead. The pig was then stuck with a very sharp knife to cut his jugular veins and we let him bleed. Two ropes were laid with a man on each end of each rope. The men would then pull to and fro, rolling the pig back and forth in the hot water until the hair loosened. Then the pig was lifted from the vat and placed on a low table, where the hair was scraped off; then it was hung by the hind leg at a convenient height to take out his innards. The heart and liver were then placed to cool after being washed. The bladder and sex organs were then removed. The fat was stripped off the intestines and placed in an iron kettle for heating to make lard. I helped with the scrapings. I got a bladder, which when blown up was about the size of a volleyball. With a few dry beans in it when dry, it made a good rattle.

I remember those days when Grandma Creola would make laundry soap from the hog tallow (lard) in an iron or cast iron kettle with an open fire under it. I do not know what else she added to it. Grandma Creola was a very small, blonde woman, probably weighing 95 pounds. She was a very energetic person. She would also sundry sweet corn on a sheet on the roof of the house. It was very sweet and took the place of candy.

Our hogs were butchered on Friday, cooled, and hauled to Riddle, Oregon, where they were loaded on a Southern Pacific train and shipped to San Francisco for the Monday morning market.

Going back to my return from gold mining, I continued my employment with the USDA Forest Service on the Tiller Ranger District. But first I want to give credit to my mother for the fine job she did in raising us three boys. Dad was often away from home making a living for the family, and mother and her parents did a fine job, and she helped others too.

CHAPTER II

Life in the Umpqua Forest

One of the major cash crops up through 1930s in the South Umpqua Valley was dried prunes: Italian, petite, and date. The prune harvest normally took about the complete month of September. My family, except Minnie Thompson, normally worked in the prune harvest during the first four years in Oregon. We could bankroll $1,000 or more. Ripe prunes were shook off the trees and picked off the ground. The pay was usually 10 cents a bushel. A good picker could pick 50 bushels a day. Granddad Cy Todd, driving a team and wagon, hauled the prunes to the drier the same day they were picked. Dub might be the trayer man. He put them through a washer and into the trayer and inserted them into the green end of the drier. Dad would be the drier man. He took properly dried prunes from the drier and spread them on cooling tables. After properly cooled, the dried prunes were stored in a mouse-proof storage bin. After a month or two, they were graded for size, sold, and shipped all over the world. Grandma Creola worked at the ranch house to help with cooking and housework. Mother, Jake, and I were pickers, among many others. Green prunes are sensitive to weather and mold quickly. It almost always rains during harvest, so harvest has to be prompt to save the crop.

One day, we boys were busy building a dam across a ditch. Dub was the "boss" and Jake and I were the "crew." Mother heard him using some profane language, admonishing the crew to work harder and faster. She got him by the ear, took him to the house, and washed his mouth out with soap. So profane language was taboo where "mother could hear you."

While at Perdue School, we had a problem with mosquitoes. After heavy rain, they hatched in a little surface water pond near the end of the school playground. Some of the parents brought a team and Fresno, and several other dads came to help drain the pond. After a few trips with the Fresno, Fred Seilert, one of the dads, saw something yellow in the fresh cut by the Fresno. It was a $20 gold piece, probably lost by someone on foot or horseback, travelling to the upper Umpqua country where there were no roads.

We used a binder to harvest mature wheat. We took our harvested grain across the river and stacked it on neighbor Jehu Wright's property. The first thrashing machine to come up the South Umpqua River was pulled by a horizontal, wood-burning steam engine. The thrashing machine was uncoupled from the steam engine after being placed close to the stacked grain. The steam engine was placed and attached to the thrasher with a belt that, powered by the steam engine, operated the thrasher. The grain was placed in gunny sacks and the straw came out the back end of the thrasher and was scattered. Usually, the stubble was burned prior to placing the engine.

Shortly after the steam engine pulling the thrasher had crossed the wooden bridge across the South Umpqua River, Ray Wright picked up Bill Ulam and me in his car to take us to help with the thrashing. Ray couldn't work. He had been bucked off an unbroken horse and was not able to work, but he could drive a car. As we crossed the bridge, a fire, which had been set by the steam engine, was burning in the middle of the bridge. It was burning quite briskly in the dry horse manure outside the running plank. We did not have anything to carry water. Ray was wearing a cowboy hat. He said, "Here, take my hat. Go to the river, fill it with water, and carry it back here. Run as fast as you can." So Bill and I ran several times down the rough, steep bank of the river, carried the hat full of water, and put out the fire. Clay Ulam bragged on us for months and gave me $5, with which I purchased a single shot .22 rifle. Bill and I were probably 9 or 10 years old when this happened. The bridge has covers, sides, and roof and is still in use today.

CHAPTER III

Forest Service Career

Continuing with my Forest Service career. In 1932, I worked on the South Umpqua road construction crew for Carl Fisher. We had a tent camp at Coffeepot Creek and some 20 men were in the crew. Some work was done between Boulder Creek and the camp. Most was done between the camp and Camp Comfort. I worked with the powder man, blasting stumps, and also hand drilled bedrock for blasting in hot summer weather. A rancher let a controlled burn escape and it created a several-thousand-acre fire on national forest land. All of the road crew fought the fire until heavy fall rain started. It burned out several miles of Forest Service telephone line, which several road crew members rebuilt until the snow got about a foot deep. I closed out the fire camp and worked on the telephone line. I went home and then to the Clough Ranch, where I pruned prune trees until spring. Cloughs had more than 50 acres of prune trees and I pruned them all with a hand-curved pruning saw.

Starting in April 1933, I was foreman of a four-man crew. We rebuilt the 35-mile-long trail from the South Umpqua River to the Rogue-Umpqua Divide and maintained the lateral trails. Mosquitoes were bad, but we stayed with it and got the job done. July 1, I went to Callahan Lookout. Callahan's fire finder was on the top of an 83-foot tree. The ladder went straight up the tree and the crow's nest at the top was about six feet square. I reported 12 or 15 fires until dense smoke from the disastrous Tillamook fire cut the visibility to a quarter mile. We then walked the trails looking for fires. A 40-acre fire was discovered on Coffee Creek. I took a 20-man crew and put out the fire. I then returned to Callahan Lookout, where I stayed until fall rains ended the fire season on October 13.

In November 1933, I took a federal government physical examination, which I passed, and joined the CCC program as an enrollee. I was assigned to an all Oregon camp at Mapleton, Oregon. The first two weeks, we finished building the camp. It rains 100 inches per year at Mapleton. Mapleton is near the head of tidewaters on the Siuslaw River. The first day on the job, as part of our crew, the foreman gave me a pick and a shovel and told me to dig out a 30-inch alder stump but to leave a couple of roots so that the stump could not roll down the hill. I sized up the situation and saw that the roots were in tight, clay soil. I poked a couple of holes under the stump and when the powder man walked by, I said, "Ernie, will you loosen this tight clay with a couple of half-sticks of dynamite," which he did. The foreman expected me to put in two or three days working on that stump. When he came back at 1:00 p.m., I was done with just what he had told me to do. He gave me a severe tongue lashing. I did not like it, but I did not talk back. When I got off the crummy that evening, the camp commander watched us unload. I said, "Lieutenant, have you got jobs in the kitchen?" He said, "Talk to the mess steward." And I did. I started as a KP and soon was a third cook, then a second cook, and then became head cook, making $45 a month. My forest service job started May 1.

In 1934, I was the headquarters fireman at Tiller Ranger Station. I drove a long wheel-base International fire truck. I also travelled to all the district lookout and fireman stations to make sure each occupant was capable and if not, to train him or her to do the job well. I also made a site survey of the Tiller head-quarters where CCC carpenter foreman, Mr. Byrd, was scheduled to build a new ranger station with CCC labor—which he did. He built a new office, ranger dwelling, PA (Protective Assistant) dwelling, gas and oil house, barn and crew house.

In the spring of 1935, I spent about a month maintaining trails on the Tiller District. This involved sawing logs out of the trail so people and horses and mules could use the trail. If winter storms had caused washout, these were repaired to make the trail useable. It also included cutting any brush that interfered with use of the trail.

It was in 1935 that I took a four-man crew, Bud Lowell, Ralph Schrader, George Norman, and Bob Harris, and we built a grounded circuit telephone line that was six miles long, from Bunchgrass to Grasshopper lookout. The district packer, Raymond (Red) Harris, carried the #9 wire to the job on the pack string and dropped it off the mule at quarter-mile intervals. I was amazed by how accurate he was in dropping it off at quarter-mile intervals.

This is fairly high country and there wasn't much brushing required. I did all the climbing. My crew strung the wire through the split insulators and pulled it to the proper tightness.

This is my memory of building this six miles of telephone line in six days. Ranger Berry's only comment when he examined the finished job was, "It would suit better if it had a little more slack in it." He thought I pulled it too tight. I had enough slack so that it would require two trees or more to fall across it to break it.

I then prepared problems for guard training school. Guard training school was attended by most of the district summer employees to prepare them to do their jobs for the coming fire season. It involved fire reporting with the use of a fire finder and travelling cross-country to find the fire and put it out. I also taught classes at this fire training school. The Tiller District had some 50 summer employees.

In mid-July 1935, a severe lightning storm crossed the district from southwest to northeast, setting some 50 fires. The ranger and his assistant were out of communication in the backcountry, so it was up to me to handle the situation. Supervisor Harpham sent a young forester, Merle Lowden, to monitor my performance. He brought his portable typewriter and typed what I did. I knew the country and I had good foremen. There were three CCC camps on the district. I hit the fires hard in old burns and snag patches and controlled them. I let the fires in less dangerous places wait until we took care of the bad ones. We put them all out. Merle had the record. A similar lightning storm occurred two weeks later, near the end of July. Again, Ranger Berry and his assistant were in the backcountry and out of communication. Again, Merle showed up.

I used the same strategy as during the first storm and none of the fires escaped to become "project" fires. Merle was impressed. He asked me how much money I had in the bank. I said $900. He said, "That's enough. It would be a great loss if you didn't go to forest school. I'll take you to Corvallis this fall, introduce you to the forestry professors, and get you started right." And he did, including finding me a couple of part-time jobs to extend my $900.

Merle and Gertrude Lowden were lifetime friends. Merle had a high intellect and lots of drive. He had an MS in Forest Management. I expected him to go high in the Forest Service Organization, and he did, as you will see later in this book.

Having gone to a small high school, I did

not have as good of a background for mathematics or engineering as graduates from larger schools. But I did have a higher than average IQ, good health, a good work ethic, several years of nonprofessional work in the Forest Service, and a desire for an education in forestry. I made better than average grades, made lots of longtime friends, found a lifetime partner, and graduated with BS in Forest Management in four years, in 1939.

During the summer vacations, I worked for Avery Berry, Tiller District Ranger, primarily in fire control. We replaced some of the old 12' by 12' lookout houses with new 14' by 14' lookouts. We had lots of firefighters, well-trained in the numerous CCC camps on the forest, so I don't recall that we had any "project" fires during those years. However, the war in Europe was heating up, and we did some cruising, appraisal, and layout of timber sales to prepare for WWII.

In the spring of 1937, Homer and Bud were maintaining trail near the South Umpqua Falls. A black bear cub came ambling down the trail toward them. They caught him and put him in Bud's pack sack. The cub objected and squealed. This alerted the mother bear and she came down the trail to protect her cub. Bud and Homer ran down the trail fast, while the mother bear was not far behind. Bud made it around the switchback; Homer slid around the switchback behind him; Bud made it around the second switchback and Homer slid around that one. The mother bear gave up, and Bud and Homer took the cub to Tiller Ranger Station, where he was fed and petted and chained at night. He seemed to enjoy people, and when I came from college a few days later, he climbed up my pants leg and sat on my shoulder. It was then time for Bud to go to his lookout station, some four miles away by trail. I walked the bear on a leash and he followed like a puppy. Bud and the bear got along very well for about half of the summer. Then Bud was following his job list and painted the outside of his lookout house silver grey. The lookout house was on a 40-foot tower with a stairway. The cub came up the tower and had fun messing up Bud's silver grey paint job. When Bud walked out on the catwalk, he saw the mess the cub had made. He scolded the cub and the cub went down the stairway on a dead run and kept going and was never seen again.

One summer, probably 1937, I was employed in the Tiller Ranger District and was dispatched to a lightning "sleeper" fire. The fire showed up in backcountry west of Abbott Butte several days after a lightning storm. The fire was in heavy timber a considerable distance from any road or trail. I was told to pick up Slick Barrows and his helper, who were maintaining trail and would meet me at a point on the trail where a certain section line crossing was posted, and from this section line crossing board to take a certain compass reading to find the fire and to put it out. It was uphill and we walked cross-country and right into a forest fire of about two acres near noon. Slick had an SPF two-way radio that required the use of an antenna some 50 feet long. I put Slick and his helper to work making a clear area for the antenna, while I started around the fire to scout it. When I got about the middle of the upper side of the fire, a gust of wind blew the fire into the crowns of the trees, and the fire was all around me, dropping embers to burn holes in my hat and my shirt. So I had to run back the way I had come to get away from the fire.

When I got back to the radio, Slick and his

man each held one end of the antenna, and I placed a call to the Tiller Ranger Station. I looked over the radio set and there was a yellow jackets nest with the jackets going back and forth into the ground. I did not bother them and they did not bother me. Avery Berry, the district ranger at the Tiller Ranger Station, answered the call. He said, "The other lookouts see the fire spreading fast, running through the treetops uphill." I said, "Yes, but it will drop down out of the treetops when it gets to the top of the hill." He said, "What do you need?" I said, "Fifty firefighters tonight or 100 in the morning." He said, "You get 50 firefighters tonight," and we did, and we put out the fire over several days with not much additional acreage burned. The firefighters were trained crewmen from the Diamond Lake CCC camp.

In 1939, when I got home from college, Avery and Eva Berry handed me the bridle of a saddle horse and said, "You've been studying hard and we're going to take you to Fish Lake for a two- to three-day vacation before you go to work." And they did. Earl Duncan was the fire guard at Fish Lake and I had known him since pre-school. He and I fished for a couple of days and caught lots of trout out of Fish Lake. Avery and Eva came back by with my horse and we headed six miles to the end of the road at Camp Comfort. We had barely got out of sight of Fish Lake when a rattle snake heard the horses and came towards us, coiling and striking. I slid off my horse and had a hard time finding a stick to hit him on the head with, but I did. I then cut off his head and buried it alongside the trail, and we rode to the end of the road without further incident.

Year 1935 and Thereafter

I met my first wife, Ruth Elizabeth Lange, at a dancing class during my first term at OSC.

The first summer after graduation, Ruth and I moved to Laying Creek Ranger Station on the north end of the Umpqua Forest, where I was assigned the position of Protective Assistant. The district had several timber sales, so I supervised these sales and burned the slash when weather was right in the fall. I went to one troublesome fire of perhaps 100 acres after a 20-mile hike to get there with a crew of firefighters. This was the first airdrop of food and supplies to feed the firefighters in the Umpqua Forest. We controlled the fire and put it out.

On January 2, 1940, I reported to Tom Barber, camp superintendent of Steamboat CCC Camp at Steamboat-on-the-North Umpqua District, joining other foremen, Ray, Floyd, and Walter, and the mechanic, Joe. Ray had a BS in Forest Management from OSC; Joe had a Civil Engineering degree from OSC. The other foremen had many years of experience in roads and bridge construction, as did Tom.

Tom welcomed me to the camp and asked me to take charge of the office, make accurate reports, and get them to the supervisor's office on time, as well as handle crews on construction projects. Walt said he needed help on a site survey to determine elevations, length of stringers, etc. So I helped him with his site survey at Canton Creek.

A new forest camp was scheduled for construction below Rattlesnake Rock—changed to Eagle Rock. With CCC enrollees, I surveyed and staked roads and camp spots and supervised constructions of this new Eagle Rock Campground, which is still in use today in a beautiful and scenic location on the North Umpqua River. Parts of the Panther Creek trail needed to be replaced, and I supervised a crew for this job as well.

Part of our job was to train these young men to work and to develop skills. I taught forest fire fighting and smoke chasing. I also taught surveying and map making. Later on, I taught a 15-man crew to prune trees. We did 35 feet of pruning on sugar pine saplings and cut away competition vegetation to get faster growth—probably covering 100 acres or more. We posted the area and made a report on what we posted and made maps for future management of the area.

These enrollees were from the states of Tennessee, Mississippi, and Louisiana. For the most part, they had good work ethics and were very courteous and very trainable.

The war in Europe was going strong and many young American males were being drafted. Steamboat CCC Camp was closed. Construction equipment and the young drivers were moved to Medford to build secure parking areas for fighter planes, and perhaps bombers as well. My memory says the camp was closed May 1941.

I went back to Tiller Ranger Station where an accelerating timber program was shaping. England needed some Port Orford cedar lumber for battery separators for their submarine batteries. Some small national forest tracts were scattered throughout the Pacific Coast Range mountains, Red Nelson, timber staff on the Umpqua Forest, and I located these tracts and dug the moss off the windfalls. If it was a Port Orford cedar, we scaled it and advertised it for sale. There were significant numbers of these windfalls, and they were sold, and the lumber went to England. At that time, Douglas fir stumpage sold for $2 or $3 per thousand (board feet), western red cedar was $3 or $4 per thousand, and the Port Orford cedar stumpage some $40 per thousand.

Then I went back to the district, working on timber sales, appraising timber for sale, and slash burning. Part of this assignment was falling snags for fire prevention with K-V (Knutson-Vandenburg Act) money from the timber sales. Wright, later a forest supervisor on the Umatilla and then on the Mt. Hood National Forest, was my falling partner. We and several other sets of fallers lived in a camp where a cook was provided. We (Wright and I) were the consistent daily high set, as square footage of the stumps was measured every day.

One day, we needed to fall a large Douglas fir snag. It was tall, had holes burned through it, and was just plain dangerous to fall. We each chopped out a trail through the brush for quick escape. Then we cut a small undercut so it would fall the way we wanted it to fall. When we started the back cut with our Royal Chinook falling saw, and we had just barely started the cut when it gave large pop. We left the saw and ran out the rails we had cut as quickly as possible. The snag collapsed in many pieces around the stump and broke the saw. But we were both okay, though maybe a little shaky from the experience.

I had served as acting district ranger one winter on the Bohemia District. I had served two summers on the Diamond Lake District and was well qualified to be a district ranger. The forest service deferred me from military service, because I was essential to the timber sales program and getting out the annual cut. Red and I talked about a possible transfer. Supervisor Harpham enjoyed having me on the Umpqua Forest and was not anxious to see me transferred. Red talked to several supervisors, and Ed C., later chief of the Forest Service, said he needed me on the Bly District of the Fremont National Forest to replace Glen, who was going to the Umatilla Forest. So Ruth and I and our small daughter, Jan, moved to Bly, Oregon, in November 1943. I had a couple of weeks with Jorgy to orient me to the district, the projects, the townspeople, and the other district employees, and I was ready to go. One of the longtime employees resented me somewhat, but warmed up some when he saw my work ethics and my skills. At Bly we had active timber sales and one big exchange at Crane Mills in Bly, and Ivory Pine had a sawmill some five miles north of Bly on the Sprague River. Weyerhaeuser had a large railroad operation at Camp Six, some 20 miles north of Bly, and the logs went to their mill at Klamath Falls. In addition, we had a couple of small mills that cut salvage sales primarily for local use. Ewauna Box had a big exchange trading land and timber for Fremont National Forest timber. All of these logs had to be scaled and most were sealed by me, the district ranger, and one other scaler. Regardless of cold and snow, we worked through the winter, sometimes when the weather bureau thermometer said it was colder than 20 degrees below zero.

Not long after I arrived at Bly, Ross, the ranger at Bly, resigned to take over a pear orchard he and his wife had purchased near Bingen, Washington. I kept things going on the district until the new ranger, Spike, and his family arrived a month later.

After Spike got settled in, he asked me to handle all activity south of the Klamath Falls-Lakeview Highway, which I did. There was a great network of logging roads south of the highway. I devised a system putting up temporary signs and ordered permanent signs. There were also many springs and water seeps—none improved so you could get a drink, so I found a stack of redwood lumber stored in the warehouse and started improving these springs and hewing out logs for water toughs where livestock could drink on the stronger springs. Supervisor Ed would get to the district a couple of times a month, and he congratulated me on the signing and spring development. We had a real trespassing problem with feral horses that ran free all year long and severely overgrazed the national forest land adjacent to the forest boundary. Ed complained about the horses, but never gave us the support to remove them. He thought we should get it done by negotiating with the owners.

Ed was transferred, perhaps to Washington, D.C., where he soon became chief of the Forest Service for many years. Spike was a joy to work with. We got many things done.

On Saturday, May 5, 1945, six people were killed by a Japanese bomb on the Bly Ranger District. Spike and I happened to be at the ranger station on the morning of May 5 when Jumbo Barnhouse, the forest grader operator, drove hurriedly into the ranger station and bailed out of his pickup. He said, "There's been an explosion on Gearhart Mountain and several people are hurt."

Spike and I gathered up sheets, blankets, and first aid kits, and notified the supervisor's office that we were headed to the site. The accident scene was on the shoulder of Gearhart Mountain, perhaps ten miles or so from Bly. As we approached, Reverend Archie Mitchell pointed the way for us to hike to the site, which was a short distance off the road. The balloon canopy was mostly deflated and partially covered by a snow drift. It was white. Near the canopy were six bloody bodies on the ground, somewhat like spokes of a wheel.

There was little brush, but a fair stand of ponderosa pine timber. Everything was quiet; the bodies were close together.

Spike said to me, "Can you check their pulses? I don't think I can handle it." So I checked for pulses and breathing. Mrs. Mitchell and five young people were all dead; no one was breathing and I couldn't feel a pulse. The bomb that killed them was attached to a Japanese hydrogen balloon that had come over the Pacific Ocean on the jet stream. Forest Service employees were aware that these balloons were coming, and we had been instructed how to report them by code to the military if we saw one in the air.

One of the victims was Jay Gifford, a boy about 12 years old, whose father owned the Standard Oil bulk plant in Bly. A couple of weeks earlier, Jay had found a weather balloon and had been praised by the weather bureau for returning it to the weather station in Klamath Falls. Apparently, one of the group must have touched something that caused the personnel bomb explosion. Nothing could be done, so Spike and I waited. I didn't see Reverend Mitchell after we left and Jumbo never went to the site. Reverend Mitchell indicated that the group had planned to picnic and wanted to do a little fishing in a branch of the Sprague River. He had gone back to the car to get picnic supplies when the group found the balloon and the explosion occurred.

Spike and I were there alone for a short while, until the sheriff arrived. Then the forest supervisor, Larry Mays, arrived, and then the coroner showed up. So there were four or five there, perhaps for an hour. Nothing could be done. Larry Mays informed us that we had to wait for the navy people to come from Whidbey Island in Washington State.

This was enemy action. The navy people needed to inspect and make sure that there were no radiological, biological, or chemical contaminants before anything else could be handled or moved.

The sheriff had duty elsewhere; Larry, the supervisor, had duty elsewhere; so I spent several hours alone, safeguarding the corpses. While waiting, I dug a jagged piece of shrapnel from a pine tree, and I still have it as a memento of this tragedy.

To explain more about the situation, the balloon canopy, which I thought was made out of rice paper, was laminated together in several layers and was tough. We knew that these balloons were arriving in Klamath and Lake Counties. When they worked as intended, they exploded in the air, and we found pieces of this type of paper from other balloons scattered over some of the forest and rangeland areas. The bits of paper from these other balloons were mostly hand-sized and smaller. Since they arrived with winter winds and storms, they did not set fires. The intent of the Japanese was to set the forests on fire, but they arrived at the wrong time of the year, when the outdoors was wet and sometimes covered with snow. Perhaps a month earlier, on a clear April day, I reported one of the balloons by code to the military. Within minutes, the word came back that I (and others) had reported the planet Venus.

This particular balloon had not functioned as intended. The canopy had partially deflated and there was a snowdrift partially covering it. It was a pleasant day, with daytime temperatures probably around 50 or 60 degrees Fahrenheit and the night's below freezing. Apparently, the group, except for Reverend Mitchell, was gathered around the cogwheel that suspended under the gas bag. That is where the explosive was located. They were in a tight circle around it. The powerful explosion and the shrapnel from it killed every member of the group.

We had received the first report from Jumbo around 9:00 a.m. It was late in the afternoon, almost dark, when the navy people arrived. They took only a few minutes, but examined the site quite thoroughly with instruments. They said there were no hazards so the bodies could be removed. My memory is that part of the cogwheel assembly contained an aneroid barometer, several pounds of explosives in metal containers, and an array of small cotton bags filled with sand, each containing two or three pounds of beach sand. If the balloon descended to a certain level, the cogwheel would turn, a bag of perhaps two to three pounds would be dropped and the canopy would ascend. The final act, if the balloon was working as intended, was that the explosion would set off some prima-cord, which would go into the hydrogen gas filled balloon and explode it.

Mrs. Mitchell was a few months pregnant, and the youngsters were 12 to 15 years old, and they were local neighbor kids, so this was hard to take. It was a great shock to the community. We had held community meetings in Bly to inform the citizens. This was wartime, so it was hush-hush to keep the news from getting back to Japan that the bombs were getting to America.

The people who died were Richard Patzke, Joan Patzke, Jay Gifford, Edward Engen, and Sherman Shoemaker, as well as Mrs. Elsie Mitchell.

More than 400,000 Americans, mostly military, died in WWII. These six fatalities were the only civilian deaths directly attributable to enemy action in the 48 contiguous United States.

Ranger Armstrong and I were commended by the forest supervisor for our timely and effective action with regard to this tragedy. I heard no criticism from the public, and we did receive personal thanks from members of the community.

I understand there is a sign and monument placed at the location where the bomb exploded. It is on Weyerhaeuser land and the Weyerhaeuser Timber Company put up the sign and monument. A newspaper published a headline stating, "Balloon-bomb Deaths Net Relatives $20,000" (Washington (AP)).

As of this date, the Oregon Public Broadcasting in Portland, Oregon, filmed a documentary footage of this factual incident in their *History Detective* TV series, and they show this every now and then for public viewing, with yours truly as the narrator on top of the CCC project.

While on the Fremont National Forest, I took five overhead firefighting teams to a California national forest at their request. Our teams from the Oregon national forests successfully fought large fires on the Shasta, the Trinity, and the Modoc National Forests during the 1940s. California and the Southwest have a very difficult fire protection job. They have flammable fuels, hot, dry weather, low humidity, and high winds. The combination results in fires that spread fast and are hard to control. They have a dangerous and difficult job. They also have an abundance of things to start forest fires, and the forest fire situation is further complicated by residences in flammable fuel areas.

CHAPTER V

Lakeview Willamette and New Chiefs

L arry Mays replaced Ed Cliff as Fremont Forest supervisor. At his first meeting with the Bly ranger and staff, we talked about the feral horses trespassing. He agreed to get an order to corral the horses and sell them. If we were unable to get them corralled, he would get a shooting order to get rid of them.

Before this plan developed, I was transferred to Lakeview as ranger of the Drews Valley District. No housing was available in Lakeview. I kept track of what went on at the Bly District. The horses were mostly corralled and sold. Spike, the ranger, was leading one to the corral when a cowboy came at him with a hunting knife and cut the lead rope. From then on, Spike was known as "Short Rope" Armstrong.

I bought a house in Lakeview, but the owner of the house I bought had to wait for Ted Conn (Oregon State Game Commissioner) to move out so the former (seller) could occupy the latter's house (Ted had to move to a newly built house whose construction was delayed) and make mine available. So I had to commute from Bly to Lakeview for some three months, with the sun in my eyes while driving from Bly to Lakeview in the morning and in my eyes again in the evening when returning to Bly.

V. Jay Hughes was my assistant ranger. We had one big timber sale to Jess Roberts that was active and a large private timber operation inside the district's boundaries. In addition, we had lots of permitted range cattle and several bands of sheep to supervise. We had thousands of deer summering on the district and migrating to California for winter range. My ranger office was in the post office building in Lakeview. The assistant supervisor, Carroll Brown, took the job as supervisor of the Rogue River National Forest, and my friend Merle Lowden replaced him and soon became the Fremont National Forest supervisor.

There are two incidents that happened on the Fremont National Forest that are important enough they should be included. The first episode, which I have written about before this, was the Japanese balloon bombing that occurred on May 5, 1945, in Bly, Oregon. The second episode, which I will now discuss, was the fatal plane crash that killed Oregon Governor Earl W. Snell and others. This crash occurred on October 28, 1947, some 25 miles southwest of Lakeview, Oregon, on the Drews Valley District. I was district ranger on the Drews Valley District and headed up a search party. Merle S. Lowden was the forest supervisor at the time.

Governor Earl Snell, Secretary of State Robert S. Farrell, Jr., President of the Senate Marshall E. Cornett, and their pilot, Cliff Hogue, left Klamath Falls late on the evening of Tuesday, October 27. They were headed for Warner Valley and the Kittredge Ranch, where they planned to land on a dry lakebed. The Kittredge's were hosting a goose hunt for these Oregon officials. The airplane left Klamath Falls about 10:00 p.m. (or later) and did not arrive at the Kittredge Ranch. The Kittredge family thought the plane had not left Klamath Falls, so the plane was not reported missing until Wednesday morning. There had been a small weather front over Lakeview during the night. The airplane was a Beechcraft Bonanza. The pilot probably planned to follow the highway from Klamath Falls to Lakeview, a distance of about 100 miles, and then fly over the Warner Mountain range another 30 or 40 miles to the Kittredge Ranch, which was located in South Warner. The airstrip at Kittredge Ranch would be lighted by automobile headlights so the pilot could see enough to land. Lakeview, Oregon, is a mile high in elevation, and the route is all mountainous country.

Although the weather was bad, a small search plane flown by Bob Adams got a fleeting glimpse of the crashed airplane Wednesday afternoon. The Forest Service, however, was not informed that the governor's plane was missing until 2:00 p.m. on Wednesday. When I got word that the crashed plane had been sighted on the Drews Valley Ranger District, southwest of Dog Lake, I ordered a 50-man fire cache, except for tools, and proceeded to set up a base camp some three-quarters of a mile southwest of Dog Lake on Yokum Valley Road. This was the nearest road to the area where the crash had been sighted. A hard surface road extended to Dog Lake, some 20 miles southwest of Lakeview. The three-quarter-mile stretch on Yokum Valley Road had a light gravel surface. After a few trips with four-wheel-drive vehicles, the road became almost impassable for even four-wheel-drive vehicles. We did have telephone and radio communication at the base camp.

We had a cook, so food and hot coffee were readily available. We provided for sanitation and could handle the 50 or 60 men who showed up to help with the search. Mostly, they were Forest Services employees and local citizens. However, there were a couple of state police officers, many members of the press, and others.

Although some searching was done late Wednesday, searchers were hampered by cold rain, pitch darkness, and the rugged terrain. These searches were somewhat disorganized and ineffective.

The plane crash was at about the 6,000-foot level, and the land was heavily timbered with mature ponderosa pine timber. It is moderately rough country with peaks, rock escarpments, and deep ravines.

At daylight Thursday morning, we were well organized and ready to go. I briefed the group on what we would do. We lined up about 50 feet apart in a generally north-south direction. We followed a compass course westerly and told people to stay close enough together to have contact with the person on each side of them. The two state police officers were at each end of the search line. We did not want people to get lost and wander around in the wet, cold weather. As a signal, one of the state police officers was to fire his pistol three times when the plane was found.

After travelling a half to three-quarters of a mile cross-country, we walked into the crashed airplane. The plane had hit several tall ponderosa pine trees, crashed in a small opening, and slid under the pine trees. One of the passengers was thrown out a door that came open; the other three were in the fuselage, which was badly damaged. There were no survivors: they were all killed on impact. The plane had not burned upon crashing. The operation went well and the search was successful. There was excellent cooperation among lots of people. Many news people were there. But then the real work started, as we had to carry the bodies back to base camp where they could be loaded on four-wheel-drive vehicles and moved to Lakeview. We had carried litters and sheets with us, so we got started moving the bodies immediately.

As is often the case, the carrying was done by a limited number of people. It was a real struggle moving the bodies across the rugged terrain to camp, but we got the job done. We cleaned up the area and closed up the campsite. We also said thanks to many people, both Forest Service employees and others who helped.

Governor Snell, Marshall Cornett, and Bob

Farrell were very popular politicians. Earl Snell has been eulogized as one of Oregon's top governors, with a great facility to attract good people around him and to delegate and supervise them in excellent fashion. Marshall Cornett and Bob Farrell both had the potential to be an Oregon governor in the future if they had lived.

This episode was in *The Oregonian*, Portland, Oregon's daily newspaper, published on Friday, October 31, 1947, headlined: "Bodies of Snell, Cornett and Farrell Carried from Scene of Airplane Wreckage."

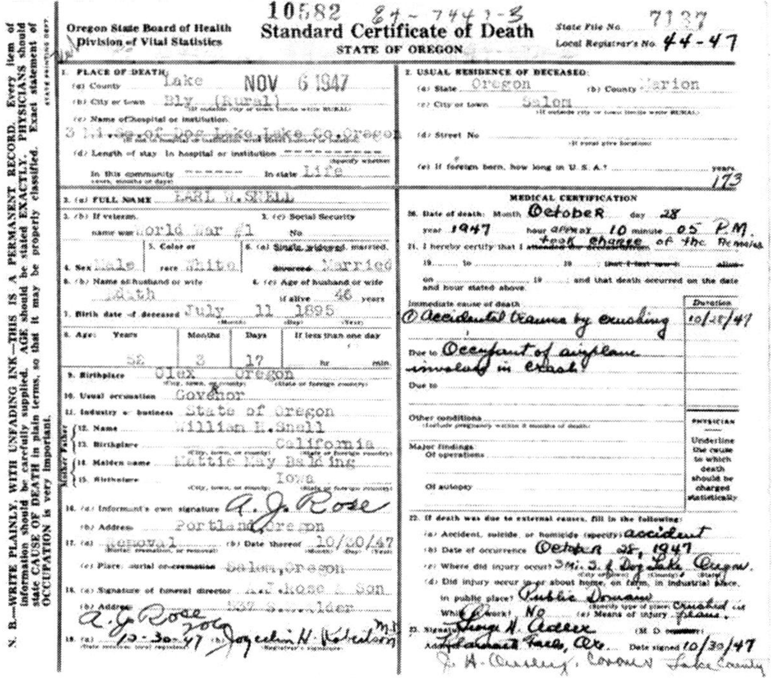

After two years as district ranger, I moved to the Wallowa National Forest as staff officer for timber, fire, recreation, engineering, and special uses. Chet Bennett was forest supervisor. Chet was a good horseman, and we travelled most of the forest on saddle horses. The Oregon side of the Snake River Canyon—"Hells Canyon of the Snake"—and the Wallowa Range of mountains had an elevation of some 700 feet at the Snake River and ranged up to an elevation of almost 10,000 feet at Eagle Cap. There were numerous Alpine lakes and many fine trout fishing streams. I established a significant timber sale program, and we built some logging roads for timber harvesters, hunters, and others to enjoy the backcountry. I was there in 1948, 1949, and 1950. I moved to the Willamette Forest June 22, 1951.

The summer of 1951 was my first on the job on Willamette National Forest. It was a very dry year and my predecessor had not disposed of the old growth slash. The HeHe Creek fire started on June 22, the day I arrived, and spread to 2,000 acres, but we controlled it and put it out. Later in the summer, the Sardine Creek fire came on to the forest from a logging operation west of the Detroit District. It burned several thousand acres inside and outside the Willamette National Forest. It was a bad forest fire year. With this experience and with full support by J. R. Bruckert, an excellent forest supervisor, I had an objective to burn the slash created by logging right up to the felled and bucked logs. I developed criteria for preparing the cutting units, helped to lay out some of the sales units, and pretty much accomplished our objectives, with only a few small slop-overs of the slash fires.

My brother Jake, district warden for Eastern Lane Forest Protection District, also had a busy summer with forest fires. So after the fire season was over, we got together, Jake and I, and decided to trap beaver. It was the second year that the State of Oregon had a beaver trapping season, after being closed for many years. We would see beavers and lots of beaver cuttings along the Willamette River and its tributaries.

So we bought a supply of steel traps and started traplines on the Mohawk River, Gate Creek, and other likely places. We needed about four feet or more of water and made trap sets to drown the beaver. We also had refrigeration to store beaver carcasses until we could skin them. It was hard work, but it was recreation for us. We caught 51 beavers, skinned, stretched, and dried them. We got offers from fur buyers. The price we could get was down from the previous year. We marketed the balance of the hides. Both of our wives showed interest in a sheared beaver coat. So we contacted a company that made fur coats. We selected a coat design and had them select the hides they needed, which were 16 of them, and ordered the two coats. We marketed the balance of the hides. Our wives were happy with the coats, which were beautiful, and we made enough on those we sold to pay for traps and expenses. Jake and I enjoyed this trapping experience and it helped us to get ready for the 1952 fire season.

One year, the McKenzie District was putting most of their effort into fighting little slop-overs. I went to the McKenzie District headquarters and spent the night. In the morning, I told them to leave the firefighting tools in the warehouse. I helped them and we burned slash that day. One of my old bosses on the Umpqua telephoned and asked me if I was changing the policy of the Forest Service.

I told him it was only temporary until we got the slash burned.

In the spring of 1957, I moved from Eugene to Portland as Assistant Chief of Fire Control. Eugene was the headquarters of the Willamette National Forest. I had been the staff officer in charge of fire control, slash disposal, recreation, and special uses.

CHAPTER VI

Wallowa-Whitman, Washington, D.C., Alaska, and Denver

In the spring of 1958, I was the supervisor of the Wallowa-Whitman National Forest. The combined forest was one of the largest national forests in the US at the time. It has about two million acres and has some of the roughest mountains of the national forest system. Sometime after my assignment here, President Clinton and his Secretary of the Interior brought 100 additional timber wolves to Montana, Wyoming, and Idaho. The Snake River is no barrier to timber wolves, and they cross the Snake River into Washington and Oregon and are a threat to the small moose herd on the Wallowa-Whitman National Forest. Baker is the headquarters for the Wallowa-Whitman National Forest.

I owned and kept my home in Portland and bought a lot in Baker City and contracted a new house. The forest had nine ranger districts. We had an abundance of timber, range, wildlife, special uses, mining claims, and forest fire problems. We had some 250 yearlong professional people on the nine districts in the combined forest. Generally, they were capable, and I would have to say, as my supervisors did, that the forest was well managed. I had a full-time job. There was also an extension of Oregon State University at La Grande.

In 1961, we had an extreme fire season and severe lightning storms. Conditions were extremely dry, and there were more fires than our initial attack force could handle. Several fires burned together in Hells Canyon, and we brought in Southwest Apache Indian crews to control the big fire. The country was steep and some of the firefighters used ropes to put it out. Several fires southwest of La Grande burned together and burned several thousand acres before we could control it. The sad part, we lost a young forester when a helicopter made a hard landing. Eventually, we put the fire out.

In 1962, I was assigned to the Chief's Office in Washington, D.C. as Assistant Director of Fire Control under Merle Lowden, who was Chief of Fire Control. I had responsibility for hazard reduction and fire suppression and was on every big fire in the national forest system in 1962 and 1963. One of the big fires was on the Bitterroot National Forest in Montana, where I was adviser to the fire boss.

As a forerunner to the Boise Interagency Dispatch System, I put in a hitch in Salt Lake

City to see if it was better. I also helped with some of the controlled burning in South Carolina for rough reduction. I also made a fire inspection for readiness in Region 3, where the regional fire chief did not accept my recommendations. All he could think of was that he needed more money, but the US Congress was not about to provide more money.

In 1963, Howard Johnson, Regional Forester for the Alaska region, was in D.C. and asked me to come to Alaska and be Assistant Regional Forester for Resource Management. I was delighted, for in my senior thesis I had picked the "Resources of Southeast Alaska." Jenny and John were both graduating from high school at Bethesda-Chevy Chase High School and the Alaska assignment was timely and a great adventure for all of us. I had been building a boat for use on Chesapeake Bay, and we could ferry it to Portland and then to Alaska.

So I sold our house and we loaded our sporting goods under the deck of the boat. Somewhere in Nebraska, we had a low tire on the trailer. When the guy at the service station fixed the tire, he forgot to tighten the lug bolts. We travelled a few miles and I could see the wheel wobbling. So I tightened the lugs and went back to the service station. He remembered that he had not tightened the lug bolts. He took the wheel off, checked it, and put it on right, and we went to Portland. After visiting a day or two with family in Portland, we trailed the boat to Vancouver, B.C., then to Prince George, then to Terrace, B.C., where our Chevy sedan developed an engine problem. There was a Chevy dealer in Terrace, but the mechanic was not capable. It took a couple of days, but he fixed the broken valve, and we went to Prince Rupert, where we caught the Alaska Ferry and travelled to Juneau.

Sea life, such as dolphins, seals, sea lions, and whales, were common and interesting. I purchased an expensive house on Dixon Street, where we could look down on the roof of the governor's mansion. Juneau is located on the east side of the inland water passage, which extends farther north to Skagway. It is not an island. There was only about 25 miles of highway available out of Juneau, but it was also served by the Alaska ferry. The highway extended from Juneau down to Douglas, Alaska, and up north past Eagle River. Skagway was the entryway, by way of the White Pass Trail, to the Klondike Area, which was a rich mining area in the late 1800s. The start of the trail to the Klondike was a steep, eight-mile trail from Skagway to the top of the White Pass. Most freight going to the Klondike was carried on someone's back up the steep climb, and the price paid for getting it carried was high.

Timber and wildlife took a good part of my time. We had one long-term sale going to a Japanese company with a pulp mill at Sitka, and one timber sale with a pulp mill at Ketchikan with the products going to Japan. Both pulp mills operated on Tongass National Forest timber logs moved to the mills primarily on barges. Most of the commercial timber in southeast Alaska was within a half-mile of saltwater. Species were primarily western hemlock and Sitka spruce, with a small percentage of western red cedar and Alaska cedar.

I had a good staff, and timber staff, using aerial photos and type maps, worked on another long-term sale. There were a couple of small lumber sawmills that produced lumber for local use. We held an auction and sold the long-term sale to Champion International, who defected and gave up the sale. St. Regis took over the timber sale, but after a year or more study, decided the investment would be too great and that there were too many uncertain ties.

Then came the Alaska Native Claims Settlement Act, which gave Alaska Indian tribes almost one billion dollars, perhaps half of Alaska's commercial timber land, and other special rights if they had hunted, fished, or walked over the land.

Our daughter Jenny and son, John, both attended the University of Alaska at Fairbanks but did not graduate. We bought Jenny a nice parka and wool clothes. Jenny would sometimes call us from Fairbanks and say, "It is 50 degrees below zero this morning, and we have ice fog." The army was about to draft John, so he went to Oregon and enlisted. He was in a missile battalion in West Germany for two years. He married a German girl, Renate, and they brought their daughter, Andrea, here to America when he returned from the army. They later divorced.

Jenny married a local boy in Juneau. His dad was Norwegian and his mother was seven-eighths Alaska Indian. Her husband's name was Terry Field. They had a daughter, Ruth Field, but divorced within the first year of marriage, and Jenny went back to Portland. After her divorce, she married Wayne Han and had three boys.

Jan, my eldest daughter, had three sons and three daughters. Her gift in music was excellent and she had a high IQ.

My boat came in real handy. I hunted Sitka black-tailed deer very successfully and killed five moose, including those taken on other trips to Alaska with German relatives.

In 1967, I sold the residence in Alaska and moved to Denver, Colorado, where I was assigned the job of Assistant Regional Forester, in charge of fire control, air operations, and law enforcement on national forest land in Region 2. I purchased a house in Lakewood and had a pizza party to meet the regional office personnel. My fire job went well. We established an air tanker base in cooperation with Region 1 and Yellowstone National Park. We had a potentially bad fire on the White River National Forest, but it was controlled probably at less than 100 acres. There was also a potentially bad fire in Wyoming on Medicine Bow National Forest, but we, in cooperation with the State of Wyoming, put it out without the loss of much acreage.

We got two new airplanes: a twin engine Cessna and an 11-passenger Queen Air. Our chief pilot, Joe Jensen, was also a navy jet pilot. While delivering seedlings to a planting area, we lost a DC-3. One pilot was killed and the co-pilot badly injured. Many of the mountain peaks in Colorado are 14,000 feet above sea level. Airplane performance in that thin air is somewhat less than at lower elevations.

Coco was the horse assigned to me in the Rocky Mountain Region—Region 2.

He was a pure blood Missouri Fox Trotter. More than 50 years ago, Ozark settlers recognized the need for sure-footed, fast-travelling saddle horses.

Coco was a typical Missouri Fox Trotter. He was gentle, intelligent, and easy riding. He could travel 5 to 7 miles an hour, travelling 25 miles a day, several days in a row, and he was a pleasure to ride.

The Missouri Fox Trotter register is still open and will take horses who can qualify. Coco and I made one 50-mile trip more or less in the Rocky Mountains. He was a real pleasure to take care of and to ride. The trip was about 25 miles each way, from "Graves Lake," with the regional forester and staff and at high elevation, where I had the assignment to write a presentation to re-vegetate long ago overgrazed, high mountain meadows on the Shoshone National Forest. He walked with the front feet and trotted with the back. He had a broken gait. The back foot disfigured the track made by the front foot.

Farther north on the Shoshone Forest, near the eastern entrance of Yellowstone Park, is where President Theodore Roosevelt had his hunting camp, and it is still there. The grave near Graves Lake is unknown, but there is speculation about who is buried there.

On the book cover is a picture of Coco and yours truly, taken in this trip near Graves Lake.

CHAPTER VII

Retirement

I gave notice to the regional forester that I would retire from the Forest Service on June 1, 1970, after some 35 years, which I did.

We sold our home in Lakewood and moved back to Portland, where we owned a home in Southwest Portland. We also owned a tree farm near Elkton on the Umpqua River in Douglas County. For the most part, we rested, caught a few salmon, visited old friends and relatives, and acted like retirees.

A number of wine grape vineyards had been established in western Oregon and the cottage-style wineries fermented superior wines. So I bought 400-acres, half of it timber and 200 acres of it red jory soil suitable for growing wine grapes. This required more cash than what I had, so I got partners. We planted 40 acres—mostly Pinot noir—but later, I sold my share of the vineyard to my other partners. We purchased other cut-over forest land and improved it. Some of the properties were sold, but we formed a corporation, and some 243 acres will go to our descendants. I also built three new houses and remodeled many more.

Ruth had dementia the last few years of her life. Our two girls did not take very good care of themselves. They passed away in their early sixties. Ruth passed away at age ninety-one. We raised three children. We now have eleven grandchildren, twenty-one great-grandchildren, and one great-great-grandchild. Some of these families are doing very well—a few are marginal. Christine has her MS in Mathematics and is a teacher. Ben is currently working on his MS in Forest Mathematics at San Luis Obispo, California. Taya and her husband, Bryan, just started their own realty business, full-time.

A very nice, well-educated Filipino lady helped take care of Ruth during her final days.

Grace P. Diaz and I were married on Valentine's Day, February 14, 2009. We had a church wedding in a 120-year-old church at Stafford Baptist Church in Wilsonville, named "The Table." My grandson Nathan Han was the officiating pastor then. It was a joyous ceremony, with Grace's entourage, Loerlie as maid of honor and bridesmaids Taya, Argie, JayLynn, and May coming from many parts of the US, and all my descendants in attendance.

The entourage dressing room, some 50 yards from the church door, opened and the girls in their fineries walked to the church in a blinding snow storm.

The reception was in Hayden's Grill at the Century Hotel in Tualatin. Special guests were Bob and Laura Dunbar, family friends dating back 100 years; Tom Ouimette and Tamara (special friends); Tom is a financial advisor. Gerald and Reverend Bettie Mitchell, the bride's special friends, and some 20 friends of the bride's.

Grace and I spoke of our journey as being "a road less travelled by ..." We have now been married more than four and a half years and our marriage has grown stronger and sweeter each passing day. I was 95 years old in February 14, 2009 and in very good health. We visited my Smith cousins in Florida on our honeymoon, and they treated us like royalty. In 2011, we took the train trip across Canada, and later this year, we have a scheduled trip to Alaska.

OHSU diagnosed me with "aortic stenosis" after a series of tests. It is a deterioration of the valve, which forces the heart to work harder to pump blood, often leading to heart failure, blood clots, and sudden death. I opted to be a candidate of a first-of-a-kind artificial heart valve that can be implanted without major surgery, a new approach to patients who cannot undergo the more invasive open heart surgery. This involves a transcatheter valve that is threaded through a vein in the groin and wedged into the aortic opening by an inflatable balloon, replacing the job of the natural heart valve. My cardiologist at OHSU did not feel like doing it to me because of my age, so he sent me to Cedar Sinai Medical Center in Los Angeles, California, because they had enough experience to do this TAVI (Transcatheterization Aortic Valve Insertion). We got a flight to L.A. and stayed with Grace's good friend, May Layco.

While we were in L.A., the doctor explained to me and Grace the seriousness of my heart condition. The doctor told my wife that only 20 percent of my heart was working then, which was why I got too tired and ran out of breath after a very short-distance walk, but now it is working at 60 percent after the TAVI.. The night before the procedure, Grace and I were in May's apartment, and we were preparing for the next day's activity. Grace asked me if I was ready for the whole process and if I was open to receive Jesus and accept Him as my personal savior in life. I said "yes," and the three of us said "The Sinner's Prayer" at 8:00 p.m. in May's living room.

During the admission process, they had to flush my kidneys, but they were not working 100 percent. Anyway, they corrected it. In addition to that, they saw a couple of coronary arteries were partially blocked and planned to put stents in them. On the day of the procedure, the team of doctors decided to take another picture of my coronary arteries using a powerful camera (I should say) that could capture at a different dimension a very conspicuous angle of my arteries, and they decided I didn't need a stent because it was still working at 50 percent. This was a miracle, because I was examined and evaluated at OHSU before we went to LA, and Cedar Sinai also reexamined my heart and had the same results, and at this instant in the catheterization laboratory, something positive happened. God is so good to me. He is surely "My Healer."

It took more than their normal time to do the procedure, and Grace said that other family members outside waiting for their loved ones' turns for the same TAVI procedure got tired of waiting. Same thing with Grace, Taya, and Andrea, who were there for me. Cedar Sinai did a very good job accommodating me, and all the nurses and other staff were doing an excellent job taking care me, and the same thing with Grace. It was not easy for me with my recovery from all the anesthetics and other medications I had been through.

On top of the aortic stenosis, I have been diagnosed with atrial fibrillation (heart murmur), which my former doctor detected quite a few years ago, like 15 to 20 years. I had been taking digoxin then and that helped me get by. A few months later the digoxin was discontinued.

The surgeon at Cedar Sinai, Dr. R. Makkar, did an excellent job of inserting the valve through my groin. I was sedated and was in the Intensive Care Unit for a week and on the medical floor for three days, so I stayed a total of 10 days. We stayed at May's for another week for a post-procedure check-up before I was allowed to come home to Portland. They said my case was a complete success. Cedar Sinai has been doing this for about seven years. In fact, they averaged about four procedures per day while I was there. When my turn came, a group of heart specialists in

Brazil watched the procedure done to me live on camera to learn how to do it. Dr. Makkar has done the procedure several hundred times. As I walked across his office prior to the procedure, I heard him tell his staff that I was otherwise healthy, needed the procedure, and was a natural for it.

The doctor released me and we flew back home to Portland on July 5, 2012. I went to a cardiac rehabilitation exercise program and did very well. Now I choose to do regular walking exercise at the Gabriel Park here in Southwest Portland, if the weather allows.

A few months later on, Grace and I had the flu, and I was in OHSU Hospital up on the hill in January 2013. A team of doctors was working on me and I survived. I had a reaction to the potent medicine I received. My descendants thought I was terminally ill, but the doctor said I was loaded with medicine to fight the flu, and I was healthy again in about a week and fully recovered after a month or so. Grace stayed with me all those days I was in the hospital (both in LA and OHSU). Grace takes good care of me through illness and health. We care for each other and we have a very good life together.

Perhaps it is my "love for life" that has kept me alive until now. As of now, I am a 100 years old and 73 days. My colleagues asked me at one Luncheon Meeting (every last Friday of the month, the FS retirees meet) what my secret to living a long time is. I said, "Grace keeps me going so that I don't have time to die." They all laughed and were amazed at my humor. *Why not!*

CHAPTER VIII

In All

enerally, my career—to me—has been exceptional. It seems like it takes about a year to get on top of the job and then you can really produce and have good results for a couple of years. Then the boss says, "You need a new challenge." That happened to me.

I want to pay tribute to some of the people I've worked with in the Forest Service. I have honored them with a donation to the museum in Missoula. Larry Mays was one of my early bosses in the Forest Service, and I thought Larry had the qualifications to be chief of the Forest Service. He was the forest supervisor of Fremont when I worked for him. He was also at Oregon State University taking some courses at the time I was there. That is where we first became acquainted. He was a very outstanding man with a wonderful mind, energy, drive, everything.

Also, I have referred to Merle Lowden; he was an outstanding leader in the Forest Service. There's also Marion M. "Red" Nelson, who was the number three man in the chief's office when I was there. I also worked on the Fremont Forest at the time that Ed Cliff was supervisor. Ed had an outstanding mind and was a wonderful negotiator and a cooperator.

Some of the other people I have worked with were more decisive than him, but Ed got the job done. He got it done by greasing the wheels and usually without causing very much friction. He was really a great chief and a great supervisor too.

I also must mention some of the other early bosses I had: Gene Rogers was a great old-time district ranger, who was very earthy and a very competent ranger. Following him, I worked for Avery Berry, who was an outstanding person. They have dedicated some places on the South Umpqua District to Avery Berry, who was a ranger there. I also worked on the Fremont as an assistant ranger for Ross Shepherd. Ross was a very competent, old-time ranger and had about as much know-how out in the woods and on the range, with livestock and with people, as anyone I ever worked with. I also worked with Spike Armstrong, who was a ranger on the Bly District of the Fremont. Spike was a really fun guy to work with. On the Wallowa, after I left the Fremont, I worked for Chet Bennett. Chet was the supervisor and gave me lots of rope, and I was really able to accomplish a lot while I was on the Wallowa Forest. We got a good timber sale program going there.

I've gone back to most of the areas where I marked timber and laid out timber sales, and I'm very proud of the accomplishments. Some of those areas now have been harvested a second time. Some of the fires that burned where I have been and where we rehabilitated and reforested are now large second growth in western Oregon. I do not have any apologies for any of my assignments or accomplishments in the Forest Service. I feel good about them all. I had a wonderful career in the Forest Service.

Getting back to this mention of the great bosses: Herb Stone was a great regional forester. I traveled with Herb in the backcountry a lot. We traveled on horseback in the wilderness areas of the Willamette and the Wallowa-Whitman and hunted together. Herb had a very inquiring mind and was interested in everything. He just really kept me awake all the time. He was a wonderful regional forester. So were Dave Nordwell in Region 2 and Howard Johnson in Region 10. I had lots of fun working in Alaska with Vince Olson, who was the forest supervisor of the North

Tongass, and Jack Bennett was his timber sale man. I can just think of many, many great people I've worked with in Forest Service. It was just great to be associated with them. I want to comment about my wife and my Forest Service career. When we were in college, Ruth and I both enjoyed dancing. We met at a dancing class where neither of us belonged, and we had both done the old-time dances—the polka and schottisches—since we were little kids. I danced with two or three girls at this beginner's class and then I spotted Ruth, who could dance. During our college years, we probably danced an average of twice a week. We got married just two days before graduation. Her folks put on a nice church wedding for us in Portland, and then we moved to Laying Creek Ranger Station, where I went to work. During my career, Ruth was never a problem. With my frequent transfers, Ruth always said, "If you're going, I'm going." The kids were not that easy when they were growing up. They had their buddies, and they often caused some family distraction, never anything very serious, but they liked to stay put. We moved around a lot. As for Ruth, she just was a wonderful wife.

What does it take to be a successful ranger, and what does it take to be a successful forest supervisor, and what does it take to be a successful staff person? I think it all ties together. I always tried to get there a little earlier, work a little harder, and stay a little later if necessary, consider the problems and consider all the alternatives and what is the best solution, then go for it. A lot of times, when you're a forest ranger or a forest supervisor, you don't really have all the facts. But you have to take the facts you have available and deal with them, making the best solution that you can with the facts that you have. Sometimes you have to go back for more facts. When you get to be a forest supervisor, it seems like your problems are never black and white; they are various shades of gray. Again, you have to deal with the facts as you know them. I always tried to make a decision that was good.

To be a successful staff person at all levels of the organization is to do your job the very best you can and work studiously at it and do the job pretty much the way the boss wants it done. I think military training does help in the Forest Service. I had two years of military training at Oregon State University; it was a requirement when I was there. It helps you to be decisive.

As far as smokejumpers are concerned, I had a responsibility for overseeing and doing some training of smokejumper units when I was in fire control. I think smokejumping is a very successful fire suppression technique and it builds young men. A lot of those who join the smokejumper program are those who are looking for an opportunity to make good money While I was in the chief's office, we developed a lot of fire safety equipment, the ten standard orders, and we advanced the use of helicopters and air tankers in forest fire suppression, a great deal during those three years. Merle Lowden was very outstanding in getting new means of firefighting. It seems to me now, though, that I'm not close to it anymore, that we have moved from the rapid initial attack by the lone fireman or the small fire crew to fire engines and big helicopters and air tankers. I think we have to have fire crews on the district. It would be far cheaper to have crews that do the district work and are well-trained in firefighting. We could manage the district business, do the work, and save millions and millions, if not maybe billions, of dollars in expenses and losses for the forest.

Regarding logging operations in western Oregon, the mills, the logging equipment, the techniques, everything has changed tremendously, because we are not logging old-growth forest. We are logging baby trees, down to three- or four-inch tops and even down to 2-inch tops. So there have been vast changes in the milling. The mills are semiautomatic and have tremendous output. I went through one of the local mills in western Oregon not very long ago, and they put out 335,000 board feet per shift. Most of the logs going in the green end are less than 22 inches in diameter; a lot of them are only 10 inches in diameter. That means there has to be a lot of logs.

I have a grandson who has just graduated from Oregon State University in Forest Engineering, and I'm not sure what the changes have been. There is a lot more emphasis on environmental issues; I can remember when the State Game Department in Oregon made us pull all of the wood out of the streams, including the old drifts. But the last 20 years, they have been putting wood back in emphasizing conifer trees in riparian zones. What we need is more broadleaf—maple and alder—the natural tree, to give shade to the streams. They provide more insect life, and I think that they would be a better cover in the riparian zone. An occasional conifer is okay, but I think that, actually, the broadleaf trees are the natural growth that was there, including the brush and so on, along the streams. I have recently been fishing some of the estuaries on the Oregon coast. I have fished them for more than 70 years. The Army Engineers do not want any trees on the levees, and so there are no trees, but we used to have big spruce trees on the dikes and levees, and that's where you caught the big salmon that came into the streams. That's where the Coho's stayed; that's where the bugs were. So I would like to see a lot more effort put into having some cover along the estuaries on the Oregon coast. It's essential, really, for good fish management.

I was never seriously injured in my Forest Service career. I worked with mules and horses, automobiles, airplanes, and helicopters. I was just lucky, and I never had any serious injury. Of course, we had Ray Lindbergh, an outstanding safety officer, fairly early in

my career. He was a good, methodical training officer, and I got lots of good leads from
him. I had lots of opportunities for injuries.
These occur, as you know; you fight fast-mov-
ing fires on steep, brushy hillsides. At one
point, I had a crown fire go right over the top
of me, and it started burning holes in my hat
and my shirt. I had to run for it to get out of
there. There have been lots of opportunities
to get hurt, but I've just been fortunate, and
also careful.

One of the greatest Forest Service stories
that I've heard was the Lochsa Ranger Station
story, where the fire of 1934 burned over and
around the station. Approximately 100 people saved themselves, saved the livestock, and
saved the station. I think that's a great story.

Early in my career, I worked for some real
characters in the Forest Service. I think of
Gene Rogers. Gene grew up, as he said, on a
pine ridge in Colorado, and his dad was a tie
hacker. He said, "I figured there had to be a
better way to make a living." So he moved
up to Montana and went to work for the
National Park Service in about 1909; then
he moved over to the Forest Service. Gene
had a repertory of cuss words, unequalled by

anyone I've ever been around. One time we were trying to load his horse, Old Diamond, and a couple of packhorses for him to go to a fire on Ash Creek, which was some 18 miles up the South Umpqua from Tiller. I was going to take Gene up there in the truck. Old Diamond was an older, well-educated horse. He was spirited and he didn't want to go into the corral. So the packer was trying to lasso him and trying to chase him into the corral. Diamond was just having a good time staying away from the rope and doing his own thing out there. Of course, the fire was burning and Gene was anxious to get started. He sat down on a log and I never heard such a string—the air was just blue around there for about five minutes. Old Diamond cocked his ear and listened, and then he turned and came and went right into the corral. And that's a true story. So he knew about how far he could provoke Gene and get away with it, and he knew when to shape up.

Avery Berry, who followed Gene Rogers as ranger on the South Umpqua, was also a real character. He was a fine ranger; I learned a lot from him. When he wanted things done right, he wanted them done right, and there was no shortcutting. He was a good trainer. Very early in my career, a man by the name of Ray Sloan and I were setting some new posts on Forest Service CCC-built roads. In some cases, where the roads joined, the county roads were changed. We were changing a post; we had to take out the old one. It had been tamped in with rock work and soil. It was very hard to get loose. We had a bar and were prying on it and shaking it and trying to get the old post out of there so we could move it. Avery came by about that time and asked, "What's the problem?" We said, "This damn post is hard to get out of here and we've been working on it for 15 minutes already." Avery was a big guy with a pretty good potbelly on him, and he said, "I think you've loosened it up." He walked over to it and got that big potbelly against it and straightened up, and as Ray said, the dust flew, the thunder rolled, the rocks flew out of the way, and out came the post. So that was an interesting little incident in my lifetime in the Forest Service.

When Major Kelly was on a trip west one time, I was just a peon, but he came to our fire school on the South Umpqua District at Tiller and made a very sensible presentation there. I did not meet Bob Marshall or Leopold or Carhart.

The best instances of cooperation that I can remember: When I moved to the Willamette Forest in 1951, I had just arrived and the HeHe Creek fire started on an active logging operation. It was late June, but it was dry; we had east winds to contend with. The fire was a difficult one. The logger where the fire started was Bill Razer. Bill was noted for being a high-production logger, but I was told he had had fires that burned him out before. So he was perhaps more interested in production than he was in good fire prevention and good fire preparedness on his operation. Another logger in the area was named John Alum. John Alum had started out as a trucker hauling vegetables from California to Oregon and Washington, but had gone into the logging business. I remember him, shortly after the fire started, getting up on a stump and telling his crew that this was their livelihood and this was their job, and by God, they had better shape up and do everything they could to put the fire out. His crew was outstanding on the forest.

We had a Pope & Talbot crew under the direction of Art Brooks that was outstanding. Hines Lumber Company, which had a strong union and cut nothing but national forest timber, should have been one of our top cooperators, but they were not on the Willamette Forest while I was there.

I worked with several Fish and Game Departments. All that I could say about them was that most of them were critical of the Forest Service. There were exceptions, of course, but the general trend in Alaska and in Oregon was to be critical of the Forest Service and to blame the Forest Service for some of the problems that were really caused by the management of the game departments.

Regarding regional foresters and chiefs: I have known and worked with quite a few regional foresters: Dave Nordwell, Herb Stone, and Howard Johnson. They were all real broad gauge, real outstanding people. The Forest Service under the old system, with their very critical review of promotion of people, did an outstanding job of selecting people to advance in their careers in the Forest Service.

I have never known a regional forester or a chief who was not a very, very capable person. Herb Stone would rate way up there, and I guess Lyle Watts would rate way up there as chief. I worked with Lyle a lot after his retirement, when he moved back to Oregon. He was a really outstanding individual.

I didn't get involved very much with insects and disease control while I was in the Forest Service. I think we need a lot more attention to that now with the emphasis on creating a lot more roadless areas. Those areas that are proposed for roadless designation that I am familiar with have real serious bug problems. It's just the wrong way to go about it. They need management rather than a lock up.

I don't know if I could say which fire was the worst I was ever on. I have been on many big fires, a lot of them in California in the brush fields. I had a good reputation fighting fires on the Trinity and Modoc Forests in California. They were big, dangerous fires, and our firefighting techniques in Region 6 appeared to me, at the time, to be a little different than California's. We were taught to build a line and burn it out. It works very well when you can do that. I did that successfully on some of the big fires in California. It scared a lot of firefighters, who thought we had an escaped fire, but we built the line in the proper place and burned it out and got a lot of black line. We got some praise from the other firefighters, the forest supervisors, and the rangers in the region. I took a team several times from the Fremont Forest to bad fires in California.

I have had lots of involvement with wilderness on the Willamette and on the Wallowa-Whitman and somewhat less in Alaska. I know that my feelings have changed some about wilderness. I think we need some wilderness; I don't think we need to expand the wilderness as we did with the Eagle Cap into areas where timber has been harvested and logs had been driven down the Minam River. I think we included some areas in wilderness area that probably should not have been included, and we did it because of pressure from wilderness advocates. While I was in the thick of the Multiple-Use Sustained-Yield Act when it was passed, we had an active mining group in Baker County, Oregon. They had been active since gold was discovered there in 1858. They were in opposition to it as originally written. As my feelings have changed about the Multiple-Use Act, I think the national forest should be protected and managed. I would like to see every ranger district have work crews. In the west, we have millions of acres of plantations that need thinning and pruning and real management. I would like to see more harvesting of the old growth timber. Thank goodness we harvested as much as we did before. We got road systems and we got some young forest growing. I think in the wilderness areas and other designated areas we need to keep some old growth areas. But the national forest ought to provide goods and services, primarily for local people and for the national good as well.

I live in the Douglas fir regions, and the way to manage Douglas fir in western Oregon, Washington, and northern California is by clearcutting. We don't need great, huge areas for clearcutting, and we have never had such on national forest land. Our average unit on the Willamette when I was there was probably around 50 acres. Those can easily be reforested. We probably need a little more diversity in species than when I was active. We were cutting primarily Douglas fir. We should have some diversity. I happen to own some forestland in western Oregon. I was named Tree Farmer of the Year in Columbia County because I diversified my planting somewhat and kept some areas for wildlife and protected the streamsides. The foresters who selected me for Tree Farmer of the Year gave me credit for that.

I don't think we had any large-scale clearcuts. That's the right way and that was taught, at Oregon State at the time I was there, as the best forest management and the best economic management for Douglas fir.

I have previously mentioned mining claims several times. The 1872 act on mining was the law and we tried to abide by it. If there was a bona fide mine, we approved it. If it was blue sky, we didn't approve it. We did it the right way on the Wallowa-Whitman and in Alaska.

The first forest rangers I worked with were experienced, logical, good administrative people, without the technical forestry degree that came in after World War II. Some of the younger foresters that I worked with after WWII were not so anxious to get out in the brush and really put out a good day's work. They thought with our high economy here in the United States and our industrial might that we really didn't have to get out and work that hard anymore. Some of us who came up the old way were more inclined to put in a good full day every day we were out there. The people who came in after WWII were well educated and, for the most part, did a real good job. They probably didn't have to work at it quite as hard as the old-timers did.

We're evolving in the logging industry, and we've come the full circle from old growth down to very small logs, and we handled them. You go through several sawmills and they unroll a log for plywood so fast that you can hardly watch it. The millwork is just great, and they handle small logs so fast you can hardly believe it.

There has always been Indian lore about everywhere I've been. On the South Umpqua, there were Indian campsites and old Indian trails. Some of the trails to the high country and the huckleberry patches up there were worn down six inches or deeper over the centuries that the Indians had traveled to them. I knew many Indians and part-Indians; I went to school with many of them. They were neighbors; we got along with them well and helped them when we could. I know of many Indian campsites on the South Umpqua District where I started. I know of many places on the Wallowa-Whitman and on the Fremont that were inhabited by Indians. When I was just a boy, I hunted with an Indian by the name of John Gilbeaux. John was an expert hunter and he took the time to train me how to travel quietly and hunt black-tailed deer. He rarely came home without carrying a black-tailed home with him. I found many prehistoric campsites. On the Bly District of the Fremont Forest in the Sprague River canyon there are lots of pictographs. I haven't been there since 1946, but some of them have been molested and people have painted over some of them, but in general, they were there and in pretty good condition. There were also a lot of them on the Wallowa Forest and on the Wallowa-Whitman National Forest. In Region 2, on the western slope of the Rocky Mountains, on the White River, there are lots of big boulders that have pictographs and petroglyphs.

In summation, I would have to say that I have had the most wonderful career in the Forest Service. I worked with so many wonderful, bright, energetic people with lots of drive and who tried to do things right for the American people. I have been retired for 30 years and several months now. After I retired from the Forest Service, I came back to Oregon from Denver and had fun for a few months and couldn't stand all the leisure time, so I bought a bunch of small tree farms, bought a bunch of residences for rentals and rebuilt some of them, built several new houses, and started a wine grape vineyard. I have been very successful with my tree farms. I have sold down to where I have five left now, with about 300 acres. I had about 1,400 acres and I had 14 rental residences at one time; most of those were older places that I bought. Most of them needed roofs—some of them needed foundations. I've enjoyed retirement tremendously. Right now, I'm trying to turn over more of my business to my family. I've started a foundation for the little high school where I graduated in Douglas County. I hope that somebody gets some good out of this. Again, going back, I'd like to see every district have a capable district ranger and have ample work crews to take care of most of the fires and do the needed work in maintaining the district's business.

CHAPTER IX

Timber Wolves, Grizzly Bears, Cougars: Bad Neighbors

There has never been a balance between large predators and their prey for very long. Most of the time before European immigrants showed up with their firearms, there was an over balance one way or the other. Any more than sparse population of cougars, grizzly bears, or wolves is incompatible with rural human population.

In 1926, when I was growing up in the South Umpqua River Valley, a male cougar came into our yard at night and killed six ewes of our small herd of 20 sheep. The next morning, he let loose with a powerful scream near our barn. Neighbors used to argue whether cougars screamed or not. Mother always spoke up to let them know that one of them did scream. This cougar was caught by a neighbor who had cougar dogs, so that cougar didn't kill anymore sheep.

Probably in late May in the early 1920s, my brother Jake and I went fishing in Stouts Creek, a tributary of the South Umpqua River. Our parents taught us good safety practices and allowed us to carry our .30-30 saddle type Winchester carbine. Our fishing strategy was to hike some four miles up Stouts Creek and fish downstream. When we got our limit, we quit fishing and went home. Before we got to the blue hole, Jake said, "I see a cougar ahead in the trail." I got behind him, but he couldn't get a clear shot at the cougar, so didn't shoot. Neither of us had any fear of the cougar; we had the rifle. When we got to where he saw the cougar, there was a freshly killed wet doe. The blood was still spurting out of the tooth holes in her neck. She probably had twin fawns that she had hidden, so the cougar probably got rid of three deer.

I started working as a nonprofessional on the Umpqua National Forest in 1930 when there were at least three small packs of wolves on the south end of the forest. Henry Looney, fire lookout on the Red Mountain Lookout at the head of Cow Creek, bountied three from a small pack by using Sergeant York tactics. (Sergeant York was an American soldier, from Tennessee, in Europe in WWI; he killed many by always shooting the last one behind.) Henry said at least two of the leaders in the wolf pack escaped. He used a Winchester .38-56 rifle.

In early February 1935, my brother Jake and I maintained the telephone line from Tiller past Windy Camp and to the vicinity of Red Butte. We had a telephone test set, and when we got the telephone line working both ways from Tiller to Roseburg, we returned to Tiller. Near Windy Camp, we crossed the tracks of five or six wolves. The snow was some 15 feet in depth and its surface was icy. The wolf pack left a significant blood trail caused by icy snow surface cutting their feet.

In early April 1935, I was foreman of a Forest Service four-man crew. Our assignment was to rebuild the 35-mile-long Jackson Trail Creek from the South Umpqua River to the Rogue-Umpqua Divide and maintain the lateral trails. This took about two and a half months.

As the snows built up in the Cascades, the deer moved to lower elevations. The wolves moved with them and ate many, many of them. Wolf droppings were close together along the trails, and after exposure to the weather, they consisted mainly of broken bones that had gone through a wolf's digestive tract. Wolves would eat all of the deer, including the skeleton, except for the antlers.

Ranchers in Oregon have built up their herds for generations. Rightly so, they get upset when they are told they can't eliminate the predators that threaten their livestock, and perhaps family members as well.

If there are too many elk and deer browsing streamside vegetation, timely hunting seasons could take care of the problem, not feeding the deer and elk to the wolves—a much simpler solution and a benefit to people.

In 1940, I was a CCC foreman at Steamboat CCC Camp, some 50 miles east of Roseburg. A recluse trapper stopped by for a meal and to spend the night. He said his trapper's cabin was north of Thorn Prairie. I asked if he trapped wolves. Here are his comments: "I think I caught the last wolf in the Umpqua in one of my wolf sets. He fought so hard, he tore off his shoulder and left his front foot, leg, and shoulder in the trap. I looked for his carcass, but didn't find it. I believe he would have bled to death."

For those who have cattle that feed on range and pastureland and with wolves in the vicinity, they will have losses.

Addendum

After retiring from the USDA Forest Service in 1970, I started a wine grape vineyard. After seven years, I sold out my share of the vineyard to my partners. The Smith partners are all deceased. I also built several new houses and remodeled about a dozen. I caught my share of Salmon, the largest of which, a fall Chinook from saltwater in Nestucca Bay, weighed 55 pounds. Over my retirement years, I owned a corporation and transferred shares to some descendants, covering 243 acres, mostly high site Douglas fir land near Rainier, Sheridan, and Tillamook. I married Grace Diaz, a well-educated, 57-year-old, fine lady in a Christian church wedding on Valentine's Day 2009. Our motto is, "We choose our new journey together as 'a road less travelled by...'" Grace has a son from a previous marriage named Ivan, a daughter, Lorelie, son in-law, Niall, and granddaughter, Jiara, and they are a part of my family now.

Lorelie is an RN at Good Samaritan Hospital. She and Grace exchange ideas on my medical and healthcare needs.

At present, my wife Grace and I live together in a nice home in Southwest Portland that I built in 1995. After we were married, I bought her a house. She rents her house and Ivan lives in a small apartment on the lot and helps with maintenance.

Photos

Grace Diaz and John B. Smith at Hayden Grill Restaurant— wedding reception, February 14, 2009.

Grace and John with their wedding party.

Ruth Elizabeth Lange Smith, John's first wife, married May 27, 1939.

John in the US Forest Service.

*Jacob S. Smith, Sr.,
and Florence A. Smith.*

*John at Perdue
School, 1919.*

*John,
graduation
day at Oregon
State College
with B.S.
in Forestry,
May 29, 1939.*

*John, Oregon State
College, 1937.*

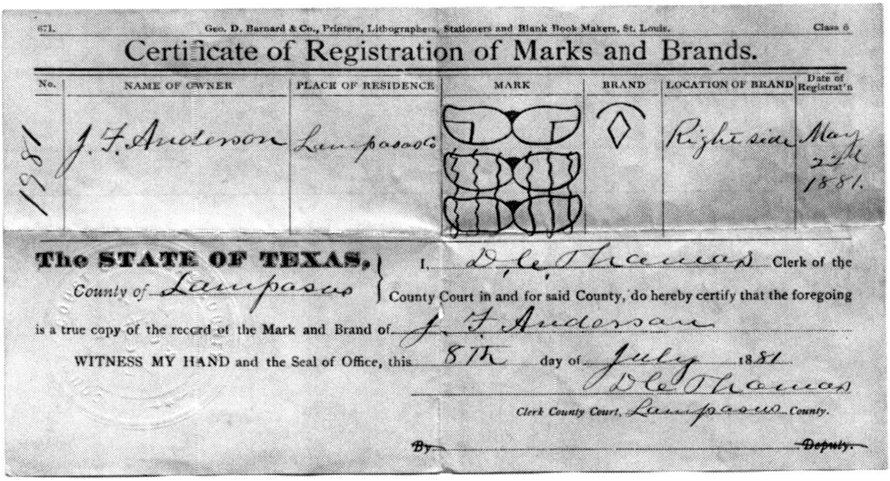

671. Geo. D. Barnard & Co., Printers, Lithographers, Stationers and Blank Book Makers, St. Louis. Class 6

Certificate of Registration of Marks and Brands.

No.	NAME OF OWNER	PLACE OF RESIDENCE	MARK	BRAND	LOCATION OF BRAND	Date of Registrat'n
1981	J. F. Anderson	Lampasas			Right side	May 2nd 1881.

The STATE OF TEXAS, County of Lampasas } I, D. C. Thomas Clerk of the County Court in and for said County, do hereby certify that the foregoing is a true copy of the record of the Mark and Brand of J. F. Anderson

WITNESS MY HAND and the Seal of Office, this 8th day of July 1881

D. C. Thomas

Clerk County Court, Lampasas County.

By Deputy.

Cattle brand registration, Texas, 1881.

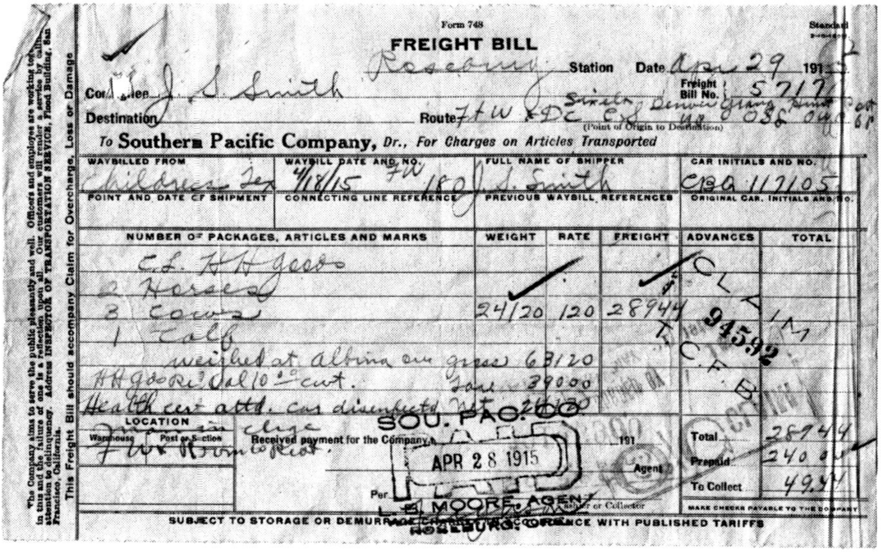

Form 748

FREIGHT BILL

Roseburg Station Date Apr 29 1915

Consignee J. S. Smith

Freight Bill No. 5717

Destination

Route

To Southern Pacific Company, Dr., For Charges on Articles Transported

WAYBILLED FROM	WAYBILL DATE AND NO.	FULL NAME OF SHIPPER	CAR INITIALS AND NO.
Childress Tex	4/18/15 FW 180	J. S. Smith	CBQ 117105

NUMBER OF PACKAGES, ARTICLES AND MARKS	WEIGHT	RATE	FREIGHT	ADVANCES	TOTAL
C.L. H H goods					
2 Horses					
3 Cows	24120	120	28944		
1 Calf					
weighed at Albina on gross 63120					
H H goods Val 10.00 cwt. Tare 39000					
Health cert att. car disinfected					

Received payment for the Company

SOU. PAC. CO.

APR 28 1915

L. E. MOORE, AGENT

ROSEBURG, ORE.

Total 28944

Prepaid 24000

To Collect 4944

SUBJECT TO STORAGE OR DEMURRAGE CHARGES IN ACCORDANCE WITH PUBLISHED TARIFFS

This Freight Bill should accompany Claim for Overcharge, Loss or Damage

Bill for move to Oregon, 1915.

John catching king salmon at T Harbor, Alaska, 1963.

John and Coco at Graves Lake, Wyoming, Shoshone National Forest, 1965.

John at South Umpqua, CCC Camp, Tiller, Oregon.

The headquarters where the author worked.

*Three children of John & Ruth: (from
left to right Jenny, Jan, John).*

John B. Smith Family, 2009

Smith Family Picnic, 2013

                                                    June 3, 1970

Mr. Jack Smith
3374 S.W. Vermont St.
Portland, Oregon 97219

Dear Jack:

I intended to get a letter to you before you left Denver, but
this must suffice. Certainly I didn't want you to leave your
official duties without knowing how much I appreciated the
wonderful work you have done in your many assignments with the
Forest Service.

As a District Ranger, Forest Fire Staff Officer, Forest Supervisor, Washington Office staffman, and Regional Fire Chief, you
have made a most noteworthy mark in fire control in every job
you've had. I especially appreciate the support you have given
me in all these jobs.

Your energy and enthusiasm, and at times impatience, with what
was being done has speeded up and assured accomplishment far
beyond what would normally have been done. Your real concern
for careful expenditure of Government funds has been a help to
me many times. Fire Control has certainly benefited greatly
from having you among our workers.

On a personal basis, the Lowdens have had many wonderful
experiences with the Smiths and we look forward to many more
in the future. Gertrude and I wish you and Ruth a great deal
of enjoyment in your retirement and I know with your interest
and enthusiasm that is assured.

Keep up with the "job list" I gave you, Jack, and I'll look
forward to seeing you in Portland soon.

Sincerely,

MERLE S. LOWDEN
Director of Fire Control

*Retirement letter from the Chief of Fire
Control, US Forest Service.*

June 3, 1970

Mr. John B. Smith
3374 S.W. Vermont Street
Portland, Oregon   97219

Dear Jack:

I have just learned that after a productive career which spans more than 34 years, you are leaving active duty.

When I write a letter like this to someone like you, it is a pleasure, but it is tinged with regret. The regret comes from knowing that we are losing a valued colleague who has helped much to bring about the many changes which have improved our land management practices over the years.

You can take a lot of solid satisfaction, Jack, in looking back over your fine public service career. I know the associations you had and the places where you traveled throughout your service with Region 6, Region 10, the Washington Office, and Region 2, will provide you with many good memories. We are proud of your record of devotion to public service and its efficient administration, and know you will continue to use your influence toward furthering those aims to which you have devoted your career.

The pleasure in writing this lies in knowing that you can begin to spend your time on activities of your own choosing. I understand that you and Ruth will make your home in Portland where you have close family ties. I know that you both will make your retirement an enjoyable and fruitful experience. It is also my hope that you will keep in close touch with your many Forest Service friends.

Best wishes for a long and happy retirement.

Sincerely,

EDWARD P. CLIFF
Chief

6200-11 (1/69)

Retirement letter, the Chief, US Forest Service.

In recognition of "Reforesting 300 Acres."

In recognition of "Reforesting 200 Acres."

John B. Smith's 100th year birthday celebration.

Blowing out the candles.

Crossing the Bar

Sunset and evening star,
And one clear call for me!
And may there be no moaning of the bar,
When I put out to sea,

But such a tide as moving seems asleep,
Too full for sound and foam,
When that which drew from out the bound-
    less deep
Turns again home.

Twilight and evening bell,
And after that the dark!
And may there be no sadness of farewell,
When I embark;

For though from out our bourne of Time and
    Place
The flood may bear me far,
I hope to see my Pilot face to face
When I have crossed the bar.

—Alfred Tennyson

Jack Smith—RFD

I'm honored that I have the opportunity to write these words. A couple of months ago, we celebrated Jack Smith's one hundredth birthday, and this book, a treasure of events, names, dates and places, flowed easily from his outstanding memory and recall. His mind is as sharp as a forester's axe.

We have cherished Jack and Grace as friends for some time, but the bond was re-inforced when we found out that our families were in touch in the early 1920s, in a little town of 250 souls in southern Oregon called Canyonville. The Shaffer family, on their way to California, remained in Canyonville after their car broke down there, and Mr. Shaffer started a little 'Mission.' Jack has pictures of their son Bob and himself in grade school. He also knew their 16-year-old-daughter, Helen. She married Franklin Dunbar from a pioneer family and became my mother. About a year before she passed away in 2007, just short of her one hundredth birthday, she and Jack sat down and had a great chat—two sharp minds recalling memories of a past, the likes of which we will never see again.

This book is a 'must-read.' It's a personal story. Events move swiftly, always factual and entertaining. Good for history buffs of the last century. And as you read, I hope you see what I do … his great family, his love of education, his concern for others expecting nothing in return. His spirit of adventure, his joy of life … his faith in God. I see his respect for women, especially Ruth and Grace, the two that God has blessed him with.

To me, Jack is one of the last-living of a generation of unsung heroes that helped make this country unique in the history of the world. I hope you see this book as I do.

Bob Dunbar
1-30-14

CPSIA information can be obtained at www.ICGtesting.com
Printed in the USA
BVOW04*2240090514

352914BV00003B/16/P